Renewing Your Mind through
BIBLICAL PRINCIPLES

Renewing Your Mind through
BIBLICAL PRINCIPLES

A Recovery Plan for Battered Women

BRENDA MCGIBBONEY

authorHOUSE®

AuthorHouse™
1663 Liberty Drive
Bloomington, IN 47403
www.authorhouse.com
Phone: 1-800-839-8640

Unless otherwise identified, Scripture quotations are taken from the King James Version of the Bible. Scripture marked NIV are taken from the New International Version Study Bible © 1995 by Zondervan Publishing House. Scripture marked AMP are taken from the Amplified Bible Expanded Edition, © 1987 by Zondervan Corporation and the Lockman Foundation. Scripture marked HGSB is from the Hebrew-Greek Study Bible, KJV copyright © 1984 by Spiros Zodhiates, AMG Publishers. Scriptures marked NLT are taken from the New Living Translation Bible, copyright © 1996 by Tyndale House, Wheaton, IL.

Published by AuthorHouse   03/25/2013

ISBN: 978-1-4817-3085-3 (sc)
ISBN: 978-1-4817-3086-0 (e)

I dedicate this book to all victims/survivors of abuse.
You are more than a conqueror (Romans 8:37).

"Ye have not chosen me, but I have chosen you, and ordained you, that ye should go and bring forth fruit, and that your fruit should remain: that whatsoever ye shall ask of the Father in my name, he may give it you."
John 15:16.

Table of Contents

". . . Shall I pursue after this troop? Shall I overtake them? And he [God] answered him, Pursue: for thou Shalt surely overtake them, and without fail recover all." I Samuel 30:8b

Introduction

I've heard it said most people during their teen years begin to realize what they want to do in life. Some are looking, others are misplaced, and still others have settled for where they are in life. I believe that a person is called by God before they are born, and given an assignment something to do for mankind for an altruistic purpose. "For the gifts and calling of God are without repentance". Romans 11:29.

Someone said that Jesus was the first social worker. He met people where they were in life and supplied their needs. He provided for those who were: distressed, suppressed, and oppressed by the works of Satan. Jesus laid hands on the sick; raised the dead, set the captives free, and fed the hungry. In essence Jesus gave His very life to set people free spiritually, and naturally. And His work has not stopped, for He has charged us ". . . greater works than these shall you do (John 14:12). He has chosen each one of us, and given us something to do against the violence we encounter in life.

This book has a dual purpose: primary is to point all people to the saving grace of Jesus Christ who is able to save them from their sin; secondary is to relieve distress of abuse in the lives of people everywhere by renewing the mind.

In social and private agencies great work is being done to help people cope and solve their issues whether: child abuse, sex abuse, substance abuse, mental health, or domestic violence / intimate partner violence. Perpetrators of abuse are not limited to one gender; both male and female abuse and it affects us all. The trouble with abuse is that negative behaviors are so inbred in most perpetrators' minds that issues are not quickly resolved, they are on-going, except in cases of death, divorce or imprisonment. We cannot change another's behavior; we can only change our own. And unless we change our way of thinking our behavior will always be the same.

We hear of a small number of celebrities, athletes, and those in political offices who are involved in domestic abuse because they are in the spotlight, the public's eye, but that's the exception to the norm. Other groups of people, those of privilege most often never report abuse. They have the means to temporary bury their hurt/ pain in tangible things: trips, houses, etc. The other group are those who are uninformed about domestic violence, or living in fear with domestic violence. Nevertheless, all are our neighbors, co-workers, family and friends, people who attend our churches, synagogues, and mosques. Domestic violence/intimate partner violence affects us all in one way or the other. It hits right across the board: it does not respect religious/non-religious affiliations, gender, culture, or socio/economic status.

> ❖ *"The significant problems we face in life cannot be solved at the level of thinking that created them." Albert Einstein.*

Aptly put and there's a plan. This recovery plan is to get back what the enemy/Satan has stolen_ your life. To help many to be renewed in the spirit of their minds, thus helping to make better life choices, and breaking the cycle of abuse. You have the *cure* to stop domestic violence in your life-your mind. There is hope for you, and the hope is the Word of God. Let me stop here and speak briefly about hope.

When I asked the Lord Jesus what the foremost point He wanted people to know about being renewed/transformed in their minds, I heard. "Hope maketh not ashamed" (Romans 5:5).

Biblical hope is not hoping that your favorite football team will go to the Super Bowl, or that you will win the lottery, which amounts to mathematical probabilities. The biblical definition of hope is "confident expectation." It gives stability. It has the ability to hold, or to be held fast by something or someone. Hope is like an anchor for the soul, and Christ Jesus is that anchor. There are no uncertainties, no failures in Him. He is what is steadfast and true.

Therefore, hope is a firm assurance and expectation in Jesus Christ regarding those things that you have before Him that He will bring it to pass (Romans 8:24-25; Heb. 6:19-20, 11:1, 7). You don't see how it's going to happen, and things are looking bleak and dismal at best, but you believe, and God has heard your prayer and He is going to intervene on your behalf.

The Bible tells us that those who trust in the Lord Jesus will be helped and will not be confounded, or put to shame because they are trusting in the Lord their God (Isaiah 49:23; Psalm 28:7). The people who have this type of Biblical hope and trust in God have the confidence of knowing that God will help them (Jeremiah 29:11). Once you grasp that the things you are asking the Lord for will happen then your hope produces joy and peace in your soul. (Romans 12:12, 15:13).

> *Hope is a waking dream*
> *-Aristotle*

Again, there is hope for you, and a cure for this preventable social ill. This cure is by renewing the spirit of your mind from the inside out from dead works to the new life in the Word of God. Let me explain the term "*spirit of your mind*" used throughout this book. (Nee 1968) "God formed man of dust from the ground, and breathed into his nostrils the breath of life; and man became a living soul" Genesis 2:7; Ephesians 4:23. ASB. The breath of life became man's spirit . . . the principle of life within him. Man is composed of [three parts] spirit, soul, and body. The spirit is that part by which we commune with God . . . The spirit is the noblest part of man and occupies the innermost area of his being . . . . The soul is the site of personality . . . the volition, intellect, and emotions of man are there. The spirit transmits its thoughts to the soul and the soul exercises the body to obey the spirit's order.

God had an original order for man to function as stated above. The spirit in man was to rule over his total being. However, the spirit in all humans is suppressed by the soul and the body by reason of sin. Therefore; the spirit in man has to be renewed in the things of God, thus the term *renewed in the spirit of your mind.*

A Synopsis of Domestic Violence in History

Domestic violence is known by many names: domestic abuse, spousal abuse, battering, family violence and intimate partner violence (IPV). "Domestic violence is a pattern of behavior which involves the abuse by one partner against another in an intimate relationship such as marriage, cohabitation, dating or within the family. Domestic Violence can take many forms including aggression . . . or assaults, intimidation, stalking, neglect and economic deprivation" Shipman (2004).

"Prior to the mid 1800s most legal systems accepted wife beating as a valid exercise of a husband's authority over is wife. [However] Political agitations during the nineteenth century lead to changes in both popular opinion and legislation. Gordon (2002). In 1850, Tennessee became the first state in the United States to explicitly outlaw wife beating other states soon followed suit. By the end of 1870s most in the United States were uniformly opposed to the right of husbands to physically discipline their wives. Green (1989). "By the early Twentieth century it was common for police to intervene in case of Domestic Violence in the United States, but arrests remained rare". Feder (1999).

Women continued to suffer abuse nonetheless. "Modern attention to Domestic Violence began in the Women's movement of the 1970s, particularly within the context of the feminism and women's rights. The first known use of the expression "*Domestic Violence*" in a modern context meaning "Spouse abuse-meaning violence in the home" was in an address to the Parliament of the United Kingdom in 1973". House of Common Sitting (1973).

The assault on the family is not a new social issue. It goes back to the fall of man. The Bible records the first act of domestic violence which was fatal. "And Cain talked with Abel his brother . . . Cain rose up against Abel his brother and slew him" (Genesis 4:8). Since that time, Satan has been out to destroy the family trying to get to *the Seed*—Jesus. You see, Satan, the prince of this world is <u>*not*</u> omnipotent, omniscient, or omnipresent. "Which none of the princes of this world knew [God's wisdom]: for had they known it, they would not have crucified the Lord of glory" (I Corinthians 2:8).

Even though abuse has gone on since Cain killed Abel, we are still called upon in each generation to do whatever we can to fight against abuse. There are many types of abuse, although defining abuse is not exhaustive. It includes: **1) physical**, pushing, slapping, restraining; **2) sexual**, forcing unwanted, degrading sexual activity; **3) verbal** yelling, name calling; **4) economic**, withholding economic resources, credit cards, stealing, withholding money; **5) stalking,** repeated unwanted phone calls, following, tracking a person, showing up at a person's place of employment or social activity; and **6) emotional/psychological abuse** which can do the most harm. The results can be in the form of depression, antisocial behaviors, suicidal ideations/behaviors, anxiety, low self-esteem, and inability to trust in intimate relationships. An abused person can display fear of intimacy, post-traumatic stress disorder, emotional detachment, and replaying the assault in the mind. Whatever form it takes, it is abuse, and it occurs all over the world in various countries, people groups, and cultures.

It is my endeavor to lay the foundation in how you can renew your mind/intellect by the Word of God. This book is for all those who really want to renew their minds, thus changing their behaviors regarding domestic abuse, and this is accomplished in three chapters: enlightenment through prayer; encouragement-by faith; and empowerment—in the Word. All chapters have work exercises meant to be completed by you the reader. There's a small piece on characteristics of an abuser/behaviors to look for.

Lastly, there are keys/strategies to be used to combat domestic violence in your life. If you use these keys which have been prayerfully designed to address abuse in your life, you will be victorious, for you have the cure_ your mind, and strategies__ the keys of the Word of God to stop domestic violence in your life. Most importantly, you have the Lord Jesus Christ Who is Omnipotent all—powerful; Omniscient, all-knowing; and Omnipresent—everywhere at all times. And He is willing to intervene on your behalf at your request or His sovereignty.

A Personal Word

I want to encourage you that you are not alone in your trials. I know from personal experience and from working with abused women and children that the situation is real, serious, and dire, to say the least. I would not even attempt to write to you if I had not gone through some of the same type of things that many of you are currently experiencing.

It wasn't until I came to the Lord Jesus with all my mental baggage that I was shown that abusive behaviors perpetrated against me had nothing to do with how God saw me, or my sense of worth and value to Him. The Lord allowed me to see in all those negative things I encountered that I was more than a conqueror. He (God) would heal me of my wounds, but the scars would be there for others to see, to let them know that they too can become victorious despite adversities in life (Romans 8:28). The Lord God accepts us just as we are in life. He then makes some needed character adjustments, strengthens, enlightens, encourages, and empowers us to go and help others.

I am in a position to serve you because I serve my Lord Jesus Christ. I am more than a conqueror, more than an over-comer, I am victorious. I am yet living to tell the story because the Lord Jesus came to my rescue and He will do the same for you. Our heavenly Father wants all of us to make it in this life, and go on to heaven. To assure us that we will survive, thrive and prosper in this life, God the Father sent His only son Jesus Christ to die for our sins. If we follow Jesus and learn of Him, then we will have good success in this life. John 3:16.

So what am I saying? The Lord does not want you to live a defeated and fearful life in this world. If you are a victim/survivor or even a perpetrator of abuse and want your life to change then you are in a good place to have your mind renewed through: education, counseling, guidance, and training by the Word of God in making better life choices. However, the renewal takes place only if you are receptive to the knowledge the <u>Word</u> has for you. If you receive these

4

life-giving, life—changing words, then your renewed/transformed mind will govern your new life. As the mind thinks, so the body acts. Honestly, if I had not allowed the Lord Jesus to govern my life I would have continued living a defeated life.

It's not by mistake that you have picked up this book; it's by divine appointment. It's either for you or for someone you know and love. And if you are reading this book, means that you are on the road to recovery by renewing your mind in Christ Jesus. I pray that the Holy Spirit will have a profound impact on your life from this point forward.

Brenda J. Leffall-McGibboney
Author

Let's Raise the Bar

It is my endeavor to raise the bar of your consciousness, to awaken your mental faculties, which may have been lulled to sleep by acts of mental, physical and psychological abuse.

According to one scholar (Werner 1982) "A cognitive approach holds that the principal determinant of emotions, motives, and behavior is an individual's thinking, which is a conscious process. Change consists of expanding or modifying individual consciousness until perception more nearly approximates reality. This is done by talking to the client and/or guiding her into direct experiences that will alter this distorted thinking."

Our Creator has laid the foundation for every aspect of our lives and we build upon His foundation. The Word tells us: "as a man thinks in his heart [the mind] so is he". He thinks and his actions, his behaviors, are seen (Proverbs 23:7). We have been endowed with gifts and talents, strengths and abilities, to face life's problems. However, when a person is consistently abused it suppresses their thinking ability. It assuages the senses, and dulls the conscious. Their level of confidence, faith, trust, and self-worth begins to decrease. Once the abuse starts most women feel emotions like shame, embarrassment, guilt, and fear about the mistreatment and they do not speak out on it, as it could be misconstrued as a deficit in their character. This assumption, although false, leads to more unreported abuse sending a signal to their abuser that it is okay to abuse and the cycle continues. What the victim does not know is that the perpetrator has deep—seated character flaws which may causes him/her to abuse, however, that is not an excuse or license to abuse. I will speak briefly on *attachment deficit* at the end of the book.

Abuse of any kind is malicious in nature. Cruelty and violence is a strategy of Satan, who comes to kill, steal, and destroy your life (John 10:10). This evil spirit uses people to accomplish his mission. But Father God has a greater mission: it is not His will that you live a life of oppression, depression and suppression. You were made in the image of God with gifts and talents; your mind was made to accomplish great things for your generation and the world.

You are valuable, precious and of great worth to God (Psalm 139:13-17). Many people have died prematurely, never to realize their purpose in life, because of abuse. Their hopes and dreams have all died with them. Those whom Satan couldn't kill he rendered them useless to protect themselves and their children by *silence* and *fear* in their lives. But God the Father through Jesus His Son wants to raise the bar of your consciences to break your silence and fear.

Fear Factor

Fear, "A feeling of alarm or feeling of disquiet caused by awareness or expectation of danger. A state of dread . . . concern . . . to be apprehensive . . . to be afraid". The American Heritage Dictionary.

'Listen to my prayer, O God. Do not ignore my cry for help! Please listen and answer me, for I am overwhelmed by my troubles. My enemies shout at me, making loud and wicked threats. They bring trouble on me, hunting me down in their anger. My heart is in anguish. The terror of death overpowers me. Fear and trembling overwhelm me. I can't stop shaking." O how I wish I had wings like a dove; then I would fly away and rest . . ." Psalm 55:1-7. New Living Translation (NLT) Bible.

Does that prayer sound familiar, is that the sentiment of your heart? We all succumb to fear from time to time. For instance, you get a bad health report from your doctor. What does it mean? Are you going to die? Do you have a severe debilitation? Or what? Or fear of losing your income. How will you and your family survive? Someone calls in the middle of the night with alarming news. What do you do? There could be a number of reasons to fear the unknown; however, we are not to live under the umbrella of fear, or even have a spirit of fear.

From personal experience and from working with women who have been abused, I have concluded that there many obstacles, but one basic reason that most women stay with their abusers is fear. There are many reasons that a woman may choose to stay in an abusive relationship, but fear seems to be an overall or prevailing factor that dictates her rationale for staying with her abuser. I want to take a few minutes to speak on what she may fear.

For most women who have been abused, *fear* looms over their heads like a darkened rain cloud threatening to burst forth at any minute. Most women *fear* physical abuse that her abuser will hurt her, and the children or even the pets when things are not going

8

his way. There's emotional/psychological *fear* of what he says, or does not say, or do . . . it's a mind game, a tactic that he uses to frighten her. You see, he may punch the wall knocking a hole in it, break dishes, throw things, slam doors and such. All of which is to intimidate her into thinking what might happen if she does not surrender to his will. It's an effective fear tactic.

There's the *fear* of being left without financial means. Who will pay the bills, who will buy food or clothing for the children? There's *fear* of losing her financial status in her social circle; *fear* that if she leaves that her family members and even her own children will blame her for breaking up the family. For most women *fear* the unknown what will happen to her if her abuser leaves. You see, most victims of domestic violence have become settled in their abusive relationships. It has become a way of life and functioning for them. They have adjusted their life to abuse. Punitive or corrective action is fearful for her also. And paramount in her mind is the *fear* of taking her abuser to court, she believes that he will retaliate against her in some way.

Perpetrators of violence understand the power of fear and do not want the person abused to speak out about the abusive behavior. They want to keep it silent, suppressed and swept under the rug as if it never happened. That's counterproductive for healing for a victim of abuse. Talking about the abuse and it's effects empower her to take a stand for herself and her children. If violent behaviors are suppressed or even denied or minimized the abuse is likely to continue. When you talk about it, you are giving it a voice to speak out. The more you speak out about it the less likely it will happen. The evil of abuse is no longer a *silent fear*. It speaks out LOUD and clear for all to hear, and once heard, actions can be taken to rid it of its power.

But the worst *fear* of all is the feeling of hopelessness, that all is lost, and she is doomed in her present situation. And if hopelessness was not enough, she's emotionally bound by perceived guilt and shame surrounding the abuse.

Fear is a state of mind due to past negative experiences; it's a suspicion of dread that something negative will happen. To address fear, the Bible tells us not to fear violence or threats (Psalm 91:5). Nor do you have to fear bad news from your abuser: "He shall not be afraid of evil tidings: his heart is fixed, trusting in the Lord" (Psalm 112:7). Nor need you fear continually being abused.

There may be many of you who are currently being abused, and it breaks my heart because I know personally how emotionally devastating abuse can be. But more importantly our Lord Jesus identifies with you in your abuse because He was brutally assaulted for our sins (Isaiah 54:3-5). Jesus was so violently beaten that He was unrecognizable by all that knew Him. His adversaries, the perpetrators of abuse, verbally and sadistically taunted Him. As if beating and taunting Him wasn't enough, with undue cruelty they plaited a crown of sharp thorns and smashed it on His head. Jesus knows what it means to suffer; He took on the abuse of the world so that you would not have to be abused.

The point is, if you are trusting in the Lord Jesus and calling on His name, then you will not continue to be abused because the Lord is your Help. "The Lord is my light and my salvation whom shall I fear?" Psalm 27:1. NIV Bible.

Now, here is practical common sense until the Lord delivers you from the hands of your abuser, you should not willingly put yourself in harm's way. The best thing you can do with a mean person is get out of his way. "Keep away from angry, short-tempered people, or you will learn to be like them and endanger your soul." Proverbs 22:24. NLT Bible. Put some distance between you and him, and give the Lord time to work something out for you. Who knows? The Lord may send him a horrible dream of what would happen if he abuse you again. Or perhaps he will meet with an ill-fated accident. Adversity has a way of humbling a person and taking the fight out of them. The point is you are trusting in God and His way of doing things: that's the renewed mind.

God the Father does not want you to live in fear or dread of your spouse or significant other. You see, fear brings about torment and shuts you down mentally and physically, but faith builds you up in the inner man. The Lord Jesus wants to strengthen you in the inner man (Ephesians 3:16). "Fear thou not; for I am with thee: be not dismayed; for I am thy God . . . I will help thee . . ." (Isaiah 41:10).

Once more, there are many reasons a woman may choose to stay with her abuser. There is another rationale that has not been discussed_ affection. The affections between a husband or wife can be very strong, even though the victim is being abused. The abuser can use his/her charm to win the victim back into their arms; thus the "honeymoon phase" after abuse. Affection may be an intricate part or reason that a woman may choose to stay with her abuser. The same is true for men as well as women. Take a look at our first parents and how affections played an intricate part in their disobedience to God. According to (Nee 1968), "Adam was not deceived" the "woman was deceived and became a transgressor (I Timothy 2:14). According to the record in Genesis the woman said, "The serpent beguiled me, and I ate" (Genesis 3:13); but that "the man said, "The woman gave (not beguiled) me fruit of the tree and I ate" (Genesis 3:12).

Adam was not deceived; his mind was clear and he knew the fruit was from the forbidden tree. He ate because of his affection for the woman. He loved Eve more than himself . . . and the commandment of the Creator. His mind was overruled by his emotions. Like our first parents who began to die spiritually, women may be dying physically and spiritually because of misguided affection for an abuser.

However, do not allow fear or misguided affections, dominate your life to the point of death! It's not worth it. Even though you don't know the future or what it holds God the Father does. ". . . I am God, and there is none else; I am God, and there is none like [Me] . . . Declaring the end from the beginning, and from ancient times the things that are not yet done, saying my counsel shall stand, and I will do all my pleasure." Isaiah 46:9-10.

God the Father knows everything before it happens and can intervene before, during and after it happens. When you begin to trust the Lord Jesus and believe in Him He is able and willing to help you in your situations. When you believe in Jesus Christ you will see faith take over the spirit of fear. You see, that's what renewing the mind/intellect is all about-allowing the Word of God to come into your spirit, build you up in the inner man and help change your way of thinking and your behavior for the better.

11

Recovery is for You: A Shift in Thinking

The recovery plan of this book is aimed specifically for those who sincerely want to recover what has been lost to them due to abusive behaviors; however, it calls for a shift in your thinking. Therefore, if you want to recover yourself and your family from a life of mistreatment, then this book is for you. The Word of God will work in your life, that is, if you are willing to readjust your thinking and adhere to His Word and the wisdom He imparts to you. This book is also designed for those who have resolved the issues of abuse, intimate partner violence (IPV) and mistreatment in their lives. And are sincerely willing to reconcile their marriage, and live a abuse-free life according to the Word of God. ". . . a wife is not to depart from her husband [except for abuse]. But even if she does depart, let her remain unmarried or be reconciled to her husband" (I Corinthians 7:10b, 11).

The Apostle James talks about receiving wisdom from God. If you ask God for wisdom, have faith to believe that He will grant it to you. "If any of you lack wisdom, let him ask of God, . . . But let him ask in faith, nothing wavering. For he that wavereth is like a wave of the sea driven with the wind and tossed . . . . A double minded man is unstable in all his ways" (James 1:5-8). If you ask the Lord for wisdom in how to leave an abusive situation, but do not have faith that God will work with you in your situation, then you make the Word of God ineffective in your life. You see, God is genuine, true, and reliable, He sees where you are in your life and how you got there and ready to work in your life, if you allow Him. Therefore, if you are willing to trust God through His Son Jesus Christ to help you out of a devastating relationship, He will. But you must be willing to go through the renewal process: renewing your mind through biblical principles.

You may ask, "Why do I have to surrender to the Lordship of Christ for my life of violence to stop? Why can't I just get a divorce?" That's a fair question. Many people have gotten a divorce, moved away, and are living a changed lifestyle for the most part; but that's the minority. Most people fall back into the same type of lifestyle: they tend to gravitate to what they have come to know and are comfortable with. It's sad to say, but abusive behavior is addictive. Most people who are in an abusive relationship tend to live in a state of crisis, and it has become their way of functioning in the relationship. Harmony is suspect and most often uncomfortable for them. Therefore there has to be a shift in your way of thinking in order for there to be a change in your behavior, and your situation.

According to McAuliffe & McAuliffe (1975) "essentially a pathological or sick relationship of a person to a mood-altering chemical substance . . ." Domestic violence treatment has some similarities to chemical dependency treatment. The "Batterer" is the primary problem focus; shelter is offered to protect the partner and children . . . Unfortunately, many partners who leave violent relationships find themselves involved in another violent or alcoholic relationship. Domestic violence can be defined as a "pathological relationship to a mood altering experience, a psychosocial situation in expectation of conflict reduction. The authors continue, "Just as chemical dependency is progressive and intensive, so is the process [D.V.] connection. The process is essentially addictive: obsessive, compulsive, ritualized, and eventually unmanageable to the point of individual and system destruction.

Therefore, for victims of abuse having their mind changed from the inside out is what will work for them, not so much changing partners. The renewal method used in this book will work in any area of your life that needs to be changed, because it starts with renewing your mind to see things as God sees them. Our Lord Jesus would not have you to be ignorant about violence or any other negative behaviors that captivates your life and draw you away from truth. Violence is diabolic in nature; the evil deeds are conceived through your mind the old nature, the sin nature that is in you, and are manifested in your behaviors throughout your daily life. It is the Lord's desire to help deliver you from bondage and to save your soul from abusive lifestyles, lengthy incarceration, or premature death. "The thief cometh not, but for to steal, and to kill, and to destroy: I am come that they might have life, and that they might have it more abundantly" (John 10:10).

❖ *Who is stealing your life, naturally, and spiritually?*

Pulling Down Strongholds

You have heard it said that the battle is in the mind, and so it is. "For though we walk in the flesh, we do not war after the flesh: (for the weapons of our warfare are not carnal, but mighty through God to the pulling down of strongholds). 2 Corinthians 10:5. We want to think that the enemy of our soul is outside of us, and in many cases that's true. But for the most part the main enemy of our soul is within us; that's why renewing/transforming the mind is an inside job-the mind. And the weapons, the tactics that we use to combat this enemy of the mind are not carnal, they are not earthly, natural. These weapons are spiritual in nature and are able to pull down and demolish strongholds set up in your mind.

What comes to mind when you think of a stronghold? I think of a fortress something that is strong and powerfully built, and forceful enough to withstand natural assaults. I once visited the Denver Mint, and I think of that structure as a stronghold for minting coins. But that's a natural stronghold what are some spiritual strongholds that we deal with on a daily basis? We deal with imagination in the minds which are: arrogant rebellious ideas, thoughts, and attitudes; lust of the eye; lust of the flesh; and the pride of life (I John 2:16). All ungodly beliefs, ideas, and attitudes in the mind have become strongholds, a fortress, set up against the Word of God. And these strongholds have become our prison. The aim is to bring down these strongholds, casting down every thought to the obedience of Jesus Christ.

You see, pulling down strongholds in the mind can't be accomplished by outside means: like secular self-help books, gurus, spiritual guide, or a mantra. It can only be accomplished by the Word of God which has the power to literally change your spirit the inner person, your way of thinking, and thus your way of acting. Yes, you can think differently with godly thoughts and change your whole perspective on life. Later in the book we will have an exercise on literally taking a thought captive to the scrutiny, and obedience of Christ.

The Qualifying Factor in Our Lives is Love

"Though I speak with tongues of men and angels, and have not charity, I am become as sounding brass, or tinkling cymbal. And though I bestow all my goods to feed the poor, and though I give my o body to be burned and have not charity, it profiteth me nothing." I Corinthians 13:1-2.

I can't go too far without saying something about God's love for us. It was God's love that sent Jesus to the cross to die for our sins, past, present and future. It is God's love that pleads with us to work with Him in renewing our minds. Everything that God does is governed by His love for us; even in correction it is done in love for our good. It is in love that He wants you to recover from a life of abuse and live life abundantly in Him. The Lord knows those who will adhere to His Word and allow it to work in their lives thus allowing their minds to be renewed and behaviors changed. He also knows those who will scoff at the Word and its ability to work in their lives. He gives us the choice to accept what He has to say regarding our lives, or to reject His Word for our lives.

You see God has given us free will and He will not impose upon our free choice, but at your request or His sovereignty, He will intervene for your good because He loves you and wants what is best for you and your family.

The objective of this book is to help you to renew your mind/ intellect; enlighten you through *prayer*, encourage you by *faith*, and empower you by the *Living Word.* The Word comes *to* break the cycle of domestic violence/intimate partner violence in your life. My endeavor is to help restore your sense of worth, and self-esteem through education, counseling, and guidance in making better life choices through biblical principles.

You are at a crucial turning point in your life, and you must use practical applications to restore your self-worth and dignity; however, for your renewal of mind to be lasting it must be by the word of God. You see, the Word of God is spiritual in nature. Human efforts are ineffective for spiritual challenges and lasting results, in trying to change your mind (John 6:63). Once the spirit of your mind has been changed in how you think, your behavior, and how you see abuse will change also. It does not matter how long a person has been in a situation or the circumstances that put them there; if a person wants to change, they must get to the Lord and He will help them to change. After you start the renewal process you will be able to recover your self-worth, and faith in God.

Now, we know it takes time to bring about a change in your mind. It's repetitive actions and discipline. We can try to change our minds on our own, but eventually we revert back to our old way of thinking and acting. But with the Word of God, the results are lasting. The Word says to put off the old man, and put on the new man ". . . Put off anger, wrath, malice . . . filthy communication . . . put on bowels of mercies, kindness, humbleness of mind, longsuffering, forbearing . . . and forgiving one another . . . and let the peace of God rule in your hearts . . ." Colossians 3:1-16.

After years of abuse it was hard for me to change my way of thinking because I had a built in defense mechanism that was stuck on the negative gauge. If I was given a compliment I would respond in the negative, expecting to hear something harmful. It was only when I began to transform my mind by the Word of God that I saw things differently. You see only the Word of God which is spirit can make lasting changes "The word of God is quick, and powerful, and sharper than any two-edged sword, piercing even to the dividing asunder of soul and spirit . . . and a discerner of the thoughts and intent of the heart." Hebrews 4:12.

If your thinking is changed, your behavior will be changed also. This change of mind can take place in the mind of the victim as well as the perpetrator. The Word will work for anyone who believes it will and incorporates it in his/her life.

Speak the Word

God the Father is able to speak to you in your current situation and help you change. "So shall my word be that goeth forth out of my mouth: it shall not return unto me void, but it shall accomplish that which I please, and it shall prosper in the thing whereto I sent it" (Isaiah 55:11).

In other words, when the Lord speaks, His words carry with them the embodiment of life and the ability and power to accomplish His desires. Therefore, if the Lord says that we can be changed from the inside out by adhering to His words then we can. God's words have a life of their own they are like spiritual warriors standing at attention, waiting and anticipating the next command to do His bidding. Consider "And God said, let there be light: and there was light" (Genesis 1:3). The ability, the power, the embodiment of the thing was in the Word spoken. "And God said, . . ." (Genesis 1:3-26). Each time God spoke the Word out of His mouth into the atmosphere, it was made visible in the environment; it formed, transformed, and conformed to His will. This is how powerful the Word of God is, and His power is still working in the lives of people today.

If you are currently in a violent situation the Lord may give you a word, or specific words which address your situation. Speak His words out of your mouth, confirming what He is saying to you, thus agreeing with Him. He may give you a passage of scripture to read, or He may give you directions, or instructions, whatever He tells you to do, just do it! His Word are waiting to obey His commands, but He is waiting for you to engage your free will for it to happen. Remember God is not going against your freewill you must work with Him.

For example. *When I was a young woman I was brutally raped at knifepoint. After the rape the attacker was pulling up his pants, when I heard in my spirit, "get up now and run". And I did.*

You see, even beaten, bruised, and violated, I still worked with God for my deliverance, and I am alive to tell the story today.

The Almighty God can do whatever He wants to do in the lives of people. You must understand that God is sovereign and does not need to confer with us on what is best for us; however, He gives us free will to accept or reject His intervention. If the Lord gives you a word for your life, believe Him. He laughs at His enemies, but He does not joke, or play around with your life. (Psalms 2:4). Therefore, it is imperative that you establish a relationship with the Lord so that you can hear from Him when He's speaking to you. You see the same way that He can speak to you He can speak to the perpetrator of violence in your life.

For instance the Lord may tell you to anoint his shoes, or anoint his head, and pray for him. Or the Lord may also tell you to leave him if the situation so warrants it. The point is, whatever the Lord tells you to do, just do it! Don't become so fearful or angry in your situation that you can't hear from the Lord. The Word of God is your deliverance ticket from your life of maltreatment.

Here is wisdom for you; if your abuser leaves you, let him. The Lord has just opened a way of escape for you_legally, and spiritually! "But if the unbelieving depart let him depart . . ." I Corinthian 7:15. The Lord is well able to take care of your every need, and He will not abuse you nor control you, but only love you.

The Word of God speaks, "And be renewed in the spirit of your mind; and that ye put on the new man, which after God is created in righteousness and true holiness" Ephesians 4:23-24. If you adhere to the word of God the old mind can be made anew by the Word. You see, if God can speak and say "let us make man" and breathe the breath of life into him, He can certainly make your mind renewed by His word. Therefore it is in cooperating with Him, and His Word that your mind is regenerated so the thoughts He has for you can come to pass in your life. How can you walk with the Lord unless you agree with Him? (Amos 3:3).

I've heard it said a man changed against his will is of the same opinion still. It's like the little boy who was disobeying and was told to sit in time-out in a corner. He protested against the time out, but finally relented, and said "I may be sitting down on the outside; but I'm standing up on the inside." The Lord knows when you are *standing up* on the inside, therefore, you must agree with Him, and want the change before it can be effective and lasting in your life.

Prayer will change you, your situation, or both.

Enlightenment: Through Prayer

"Arise, Shine; for thy light is come, and the glory of the Lord is risen upon thee." Isaiah 60:1.

I pray for "The eyes of your understanding being enlightened; that ye may know what is the hope of his calling, and what the riches of the glory of his inheritance in the saints," Ephesians 1:18. In other words, to have your spiritual eyes open means to have insight into the realization, of what God the Father has called you to do in this life. And you find out by having your mind enlightened with spiritual understanding through prayer and worship. It is in prayer that you learn to hear from God the Father. He leads and guides you in His Word and reveals to you the things He is talking to you about in your life. And if you have a spiritual ear to hear you can perceive His voice actually speaking to you in your spirit/mind. But it all comes from being enlighten, having your mind elevated to hear from Him.

In the Old Testament the word enlightenment comes from the word light, *owr* in Greek. It means brightness, illumination. It is the Lord's desire that the eyes of your mind be open to spiritual light and reality that will actually change your character and way of life. (HGSB), KJV.

There are times in prayer when you must still your soul to hear from the God of heaven and earth "Be still, and know that I am God: I will be exalted among the heathen I will be exalted in the earth." Psalm 46:10. "The people who walked in darkness have seen a great Light; those who dwelt in the land of intense darkness and the shadow of death, upon them has the Light shined." Isaiah 9:2. Amplified Bible. By virtue of sin a lot of people are still walking in *darkness,* darkness being a metaphor for sin. There are many who refuse to see the light of the Word of God speaking to them in their violent situation, either by unbelief in God the Son, or blatant disobedience in Him; either way is detrimental to your well-being and your natural and spiritual life.

21

Arise up for the Light, God's brightness; His revelation of His Word has come to bring *you* out of darkness-sin. God the Father has a hope, an expectation, a particular destination for you to reach, and He never intended for you to walk in darkness about who you are in Him or about your life. It is not the Lord's will that you continue to live in abusive relationships. The Lord has given you the ability to be what He has called you to be in this life. God the Father has given you His Word to use to have your spiritual eyes enlightened, opened to what He is saying to you. This understanding comes from your relationship with the Lord, and His Word.

Palal in the Old Testament means pray, exhortation, it means to pray now! The essential meaning is a two-way street of communication. It's a posture of submission to [a higher authority]. Also prayer is t'Phillah it means to pray to God to intervene, to intercede, and make supplication. It has been said that the Lord will not do anything except by prayer. Prayers are God's way for us to talk with Him, and in turn He will answer us by His Word and intervening in our affairs.

Prayer will work if you work the principle of prayer. God always takes the initiative in communicating with His people. God wanted to talk with His people as far back as in the Garden of Eden (Gen. 3:8). God talked to Noah (Genesis. 6:8), and He had an on-going dialogue with Abram; "Get thee out of thy country, and from thy kindred, and from thy father's house, unto a land that I will show thee . . ." Genesis. 12. God always takes the initiative in communicating with His people and it's always for their good and the good of mankind. Prayer in a straightforward form is nothing more than talking with our heavenly Father. When we pray the Father wants us to obey His words. "If ye will obey thy voice indeed, and keep my covenant, then ye shall be a peculiar treasure unto me above all people; for all the earth is mine." Exodus. 19:5. As you can see prayer, and obedience to God is of paramount importance to Him.

Prayer works for anyone who does it on a consistent basis. It is a principle and it works. We must work the principle, and praying is the only way to learn to pray. The New Testament tells us we are to always pray and not to faint (Luke 18:1). Again praying is communication with our heavenly Father. Jesus taught His disciples a model prayer. Matthew 6:9-13. And Jesus Himself prayed daily to God the Father (John 17:15, 20). If Jesus who is God incarnate (God in the flesh) had to work the principle of prayer while on this earth, then what about you and me?

Now there are many schools of thought on how one should pray: standing, kneeling, prostrate, sitting or lying in bed, the point is to pray, and pray always. That means you can talk to the Father while doing housework, at your computer, walking, or wherever you are. The important thing to remember in praying is the posture of the heart. That is, the heart must be in submission to God.

Therefore, we humble ourselves before His mighty throne of grace seeking an audience with God the Father. You can tell your heavenly Father what's going on in your life, the abuse and your feeling about it, your feeling about your abuser, and what you want to happened in the relationship.

This is your part in the process. What do you say to a Holy God? First you acknowledge that He is a Holy God, and humble yourself before Him. I have read somewhere an acronym for praying. It is the word ACTS: **Adoration, Confession, Thanksgiving, and Supplication**. You can start off by given God **Adoration**, telling Him of your love for Him, and reverence for who He is. **Confession** is confessing your faults and sins, agree with God that you have missed the mark. **Thanksgiving**, is thanking God for Who He is in your life, thanking Him for all He has done for you and yours, and thanking God for life. **Supplication** is praying for your needs, and the needs of others. It's talking to God about your problems, hopes, dreams, and desires. It is talking to God about what is going on in your life and the lives of others, and asking God to intervene on their behalf. This acronym is a way to start your prayers, and in time will lead you farther in prayer as you become more acquainted with your heavenly Father.

You pray by praying, so start off by just talking to God the Father, and if you have not spoken to Him in a long time you may want to do a little ground work, by acknowledging who He is and thanking Him for what He has done for you. You see, He has not allowed you to die in your trespasses and sins.

If you are currently in or have been in an abusive relationship and are alive today thank the Lord. Confess your trespasses, and the iniquities of your heart. That information in itself should humble you before His presence. Tell Him why you have not been praying to Him; tell Him if you are angry with Him, or with yourself, your abuser or whomever, or even if you feel it was hopeless to pray. Whatever your thoughts voice them out to the Father, because He knows all about your sorrow and the burdens you have being carrying. It's time to let God have all your problems, so He can work them out for you—His way (Matthew 11:28-30).

Hence, the first step in renewing your mind and strengthening your relationship with your heavenly Father is through the intimate form of prayer. You have the ability to improve your whole life spiritually and naturally.

❖ *Praying is not as hard as we make it. Whisper prayers during the day, and you are in communication with the Father.* "Pray without ceasing" I Thessalonians 5:17.

A Changed Life: My Heart is Fixed

If you are reading this book there are some things that you want changed in your life. Whatever situations that are going on, trials, problems, or issues that are confronting you, the Lord God can help you overcome your concerns. But there is something you must do. You must have made up mind. Your heart needs to be fixed in the matter that you have before the Lord, and walk in obedience to the Word of God. What's the use of praying and not obeying what the Lord God is talking to you about?

Take a look at Jesus He is always our best example. Jesus didn't have to renew His mind because He was perfect. However, Jesus had to become obedient in his human flesh. "Though he were a Son yet learned he obedience by the things which he suffered." Hebrews 5:8. Jesus didn't retaliated when people said evil things against Him. For instance they said He was a winebibber, a gluttony, He had a devil, He was a blasphemer (Matt.11:29; Lk.7:34). Can you believe it they were talking about God Himself!? Jesus didn't react to His haters, and He didn't give His powers to others because He knew who He was.

What Jesus is saying to you is to re-think how you react in any given situation. Re-think how you see yourself, and your self-worth. You know that you are not the evil names an abuser calls you so don't react to those names. Stop giving your power over to your abuser. You see, even though Jesus was God, His divinity was veiled He was embodied in human flesh while here on earth. If Jesus Himself had to pray and obey the Father in order for God's will to work in His life what about you and me?

In order for you to benefit from the Word of God you must be obedient to His words. To obey means to hear spiritually and intellectually and to do whatever is being asked of you (Numbers 24:4). Let's just suppose; what if, in prayer, the Lord told you to leave your abuser. What would you do? Would you reject the request by denying that you had heard from the Lord, or would you pack your bags and leave? New scenario; again, while in prayer the Lord starts to show you yourself and your spouse and how your marriage can be saved if you follow His directions. Would you listen and obey the Lord, or deny His intervening in your life? It all has to do with a change of heart, how you see the Lord, yourself and your relationship with Him. You must have made up your mind to want change to come.

Wishy-Washy Thinking

Are you currently in an abusive relationship and want it to change? If you have made up your mind, if your heart is fixed; and settled in the matter, then pray to the Father about it and follow His directions for you. You see, God is not into wishy-washy thinking. He calls it a double mind. A double-minded man is unsettled in all his ways (James 1:8). It's been said that an abused woman may change her mind many times before actually leaving her abuser. The Lord is not trying to push or rush you into making unwanted decisions, but He wants you to know what you want. But if you don't know what you want; and are confused, perplexed, and baffled about what's going on in your life, then asked the Lord to help you in your thinking process to sort it all out and to show you what is right for you.

You see, when it comes to marital matters, close intimate relationships between a man and a woman, love and hate can be closely intertwined, especially in violent, abusive situations; and only the Lord knows what's best for you. Tell the Lord if you really want out of the relationship, or if you really want to stay in it and try to work things out and He will help you. But if He tells you to leave it is best that you leave, because God knows what will happen in the future if you stay. Therefore, listen to His counsel, He knows the end of a thing before it happens!

Continue praying and trusting the Lord and you will see a change in you and how you relate to your abuser. "The effectual fervent prayers of a righteous man availeth much." James 5:16b. There's no use in talking about leaving, or talking about "doing better" and you are not praying about the matter, because, strength comes through prayer. And you can only do so much reading about prayer. So when it comes to practicing prayer and, conjecture, speculation, theories on prayer choose practice every time and God will bless your efforts.

You may have been in your situation for many years, and things look as if they will never change. I am here to tell you that if you pray and believe the Lord then He will intervene in your situation. Here's a caveat, a warning: you must be patient with the Lord, your situation didn't turn sour overnight. God is not a mystical genie or a magician, He is God and He works in the hearts and affairs of people (Proverbs 21:1). Yes, He can intervene and give you sweet success; however, you must be ready and willing to receive His interventions when He presents them to you.

Sharing from Life

My sister tells a humorous story. She and her husband were arguing, when her husband raised his hand to hit her, it got stuck in that upright strike position. Her husband started to cry out in agony and acute pain. She had to help release the arm that had planned to strike her. Oh, the poetic justice of God who can match His wit? God can intervene in your situation, even sending angels to deliver you, but what have you learned? How will you handle the situation the next time, or the next relationship.

If you direct your conversation to your heavenly Father you are praying. I often tell people pray or talk to the Father as they would a friend, but with reverence of course_ after all you are talking to God. If you are going through trials with your spouse, significant other or family member talk to the Father about it. Learn to get the Lord's perspective on the matter it may be something that you are doing wrong (heaven forbid!). You don't like to think that you may be doing something wrong in the relationship because you see yourself as the victim in the matter.

I remember going to the Lord about my husband and telling Jesus all the things that I thought my husband was doing "Lord he's doing such and such . . . this and that," then in the middle of my conversation, I heard '*Stop*." The Lord told me that those are the things that I would be doing if I were not following Him. I gasped . . . me? I was crushed, humiliated, and so ashamed of myself that I cried. So we are not so innocent before the Lord who reads our hearts like a book, and before the thought is even formed in our minds He knows what we are thinking.

I shared that glimpse of life because I felt the Holy Spirit wanted you to know that sometimes we wear the victim's label like a badge of honor thinking that we have done nothing wrong. You may even feel comfortable in your *victim* status, and love to sing the "*somebody done me wrong*" song. Or could it be that you were walking in disobedience when you got married? The Word tells us not to marry an unbeliever, consider, "Be ye not unequally yoked together with unbelievers: for what fellowship hath righteousness with unrighteousness? And what communion hath light with darkness?" 2 Corinthians 6:14. Yet we do marry unbelievers, and suffer the consequences for it. In essence you may have opened a door for Satan and his cohorts to walk into your life and wreck havoc in your marriage. The Lord Jesus tells us "Not everyone that saith unto me, Lord, Lord, shall enter into the kingdom of heaven: but he that doeth the will of my Father which is in heaven." Matthew 7:21.

Alright, so you made a mistake, or were outwardly disobedient to the Lord. You walked into this relationship with your eyes wide—open. So, what are you to do now? Go to the Lord in prayer and tell Him about what's going on in your life, then follow His instructions because the Lord will not lead you astray. The Lord may tell you that the person is not right for you and you should leave. "Oh, no", you say, "I can't leave, because the Lord hates divorce". Yes he does, but He loves you more, and wants you safe to live out your life in Him.

And God knows what will happen if you stay because He knows you and what you are capable of doing when pushed, as well as your partner/spouse. You see, there are many men and women in prison today, and others in their graves because they didn't know what others were capable of doing. But God knew, and when He says to leave __ leave!

If you talk to God the Father He will talk back to you, prayer is two-way communication. God not only hears what you are saying He hears what you are not saying. He knows the heart, the very thoughts of the mind, and He gets down to the real source of the matter for both parties involved. You see, in the above instance with my husband, I thought that God was on my side even though I was thinking, and saying things that were untrue. But I found that God is for what is right, good, and honest, and my thoughts, and behaviors were anything but right.

He Speaks

"He speaks on and on . . . in 10,000 tongues He speaks. With signs and wonders, fire and thunder, He speaks. He speaks in the valley deep and on mountain peaks . . . He speaks." McGibboney, B. Come and Dine with Me.

God speaks through circumstances, situations, dreams, revelations, nature and various ways. The point is God is always speaking. But how does God speak to me you may ask. God the Father speaks in countless ways as stated, but primarily He speaks through His written Word the logos from the Bible, and rhema words denoting the operative or all—powerful Word of God. Rhema stands for the subject matter of the thing which is spoken about (Acts 10:37; II Corinthians 13:1). Rhema may sound audible in your head, or someone speaking may unknowingly say something that pertains directly to your situation. The point is rhema words speak to a particular subject matter in your heart, or what's confronting you now in your life. For instance; The Lord may have been talking to you about a separation from your spouse. A week later your employer in a meeting states that he/she received word that there's an opening in the company in another state, and need someone who's willing to move there. Voila! That's your rhema word, it's exactly what you have been thinking about and what the Lord has been talking to your about. It's a right-now word for your situation.

In essence prayer is about communication with God the Father. I've heard it said that God won't do anything except it's by prayer. If Jesus had to pray, then what about you and me? (Matthew 14:23; Mark 14:32; Luke 5:16, 6:12; John 17:20; Col. 1:3). So, think about it. You have the cure for your domestic violence _ your mind. Take time to communicate with your heavenly Father and He will lead and guide you in the right direction.

Shifting Gears

Let's shift gears now and do some work. Depending on your relationship with the Lord select the appropriate area from the following sections and fill in the blanks.

Remember you are enlightening your mind by
praying to God the Father.

Father God I thank and praise You for:

_____
_____
_____
_____
_____
_____
_____
_____
_____
_____
_____
_____
_____
_____
_____
_____
_____
_____
_____
_____
_____
_____
_____

God I really don't know where to start it's been so long since I've spoken with You:

_____
_____
_____
_____
_____
_____
_____
_____
_____
_____
_____
_____
_____

Lord God I don't know You, but I want to know You. "Except a man be born again he cannot see the kingdom of God." John 3:3. And "For God so loved the world that he gave his only begotten Son that whosoever believeth in him should not perish but have everlasting life." John 3:16.

_____
_____
_____
_____
_____
_____
_____
_____
_____
_____
_____
_____
_____
_____

*"Believe in the Lord your God, so shall ye be
established; believer his prophets, so shall ye prosper."*
II Chronicles 20:20b

Encouragement: By Faith

*"But without faith it is impossible to please him: for he
that cometh to God must believe that he is, and that he is
a rewarder of them that diligently seek him."*
Hebrews 11:6

The rule in God's kingdom is that we are to encourage ourselves in Him. The word encourage is Chazaq. It is **courage,** or to encourage, it means to make strong, make firm, to support, to harden, to be confirmed. (HGSB), Lexical Aid to the Old Testament.

I am taking a story from the Bible of David in the Old Testament. There were many times when David had to encourage himself in the Lord. At this particular time he was on the run from King Saul, and hiding out with the enemy the Philistines in Ziglag. While David and his men were out warring against other tribes, the Amalekites came and raided Ziglag, burned it down and took all the women and children of David and his men captive. David's men were so devastated that they cried until they couldn't cry anymore. Then they talked about stoning him to death, because their families had been captured. But David *encouraged* himself in the Lord. "David inquired at the Lord, and saying, Shall I pursue after this troop?" I Samuel 30:1-8. The Lord answered David and said to pursue and he would recover all. The point is when you have what I call the *dark night of the soul* you have to encourage yourself in the Lord, and hear from Him. This is not time to wallow in your pain and feel hopeless. Get to the Lord for help. The Lord knows when you are in dire straits and He will assist you and tell your what to do.

The Word of God will work in your life if you will allow it to work. The concern is most people refuse to allow the Word of God to work in their lives. They assume that they can handle the problem of domestic violence/ intimate partner violence by their own wit.

The problem with that assumption is that it has not worked by man's wit in thousands of years. As mentioned earlier domestic abuse is spiritual in nature, and it has to be approached from a spiritual perspective. You see this is not just an American problem; it's global in nature, affecting people all over the world. People from different cultural and ethnic groups may call it by different names, and attach cultural stipulations to it. Nevertheless, control manipulation, sexual assaults, psychological, and physical violence of people by any other name is still the same—abuse. A skunk by any other name still smells the same!

And again we will go to the Bible for our standards. God **encouraged** Joshua "As I was with Moses, so I will be with thee: I will not fail thee, nor forsake thee. Be strong and of good **courage** . . . Only be thou strong and very **courageous** . . . Joshua 1:6,7. The Lord wants you to **encourage** yourselves in Him and in His Word and He will help you resolve the issues in your life that will be best for all concerned.

- ❖ I recommend the psalms for anyone who is going through rough times. I call the psalms God's remedy to the blues. The point is to encourage yourself in the Lord.

- ❖ "Encouragement is like peanut butter on bread. If you spread it around, it just helps things stick together better." Evans (2009).

- ❖ "Encourage one another. Many times a word of praise or thanks or appreciation of cheer has kept people on their feet". Charles Swindoll (2010).

We are not immune to trials in our lives. They will come whether we have done anything wrong or not. Problems comes to the saints and sinners alike; both rich and poor; the educated and the un-educated, to all people in all parts of the world. That's because we are sinful people living with other sinful people, and things are going to happen to us (I Peter 4:12). But the Lord God does not want you to sit and wallow in self-pity; He wants you to take positive action, become proactive, and encourage yourself, because He is with you in your endeavors (Isaiah. 41:10). The Lord does not want you in a relationship that is full of violence, and fear.

Your home should not have to be a war-zone where you and your children are casualties of war being waged by your spouse. It is the strategy of the enemy/Satan to put you and your spouse at odds against each other, divide and conquer is still his strategy. But "The eternal God is thy refuge, and underneath are the everlasting arms: and he shall thrust out the enemy from before thee . . ." Deuteronomy 27. While the Lord God is working things out for you, while you are renewing your mind in the Word of God and living according to the Word, learn to encourage yourself when things are not going well for you. Learn to inspire yourself and others to do something that will help others.

If you are down and out, think about others who are less fortunate than you, yes, there are others who are at a worse disadvantage than you are. Learn, and teach others that you receive hope in God and His Word. "Lift up your heads all ye gates and be lifted up you everlasting doors and the King of glory shall come in . . . The Lord of Host He is the King of glory." Psalm 24:7,10.

Oops There Goes My Crutch

There are some people who use others as their crutch. "Many people never develop a good sense of self-esteem because they give others too much power over them. They are not living in and of themselves." The author continues "Instead they are always with and around others. They are not at rest in themselves but obtain their self-awareness solely from others: from other's goodwill, praise, kindness, and affirmation. They are unable to demarcate themselves from other people. They lack self-definition." (Gruen 1995).

The Lord wants to take away your crutch. It's not that He does not want you to have close intimate friends. He does not want people to define who you are. God does not want you to get your self-worth from others. People will build you up one day and tear you down the same day. But He wants to encourage you and build you up in your inner self. Consider "that he would grant you according to the riches of his glory to be strengthened with might by his Spirit in the inner man . . ." Eph. 3:16. The Lord wants your spirit to be built up in Him so you will know who you are and have a healthy self-image, and self-respect for yourself.

But heavens forbid if you are using your pain as your crutch, something that you nourish; and hold to pacify your victim mentality. "Self-respect . . . means knowing that you are worth something. It means being convinced of your own dignity and value of your uniqueness as a person. It is the sign of your self, of your real being, all of your God-given image." (Gruen, 1995).

So what am I saying? You can't hide behind others; you can't make others your total life; or allow them to define who you are. If so, you will become dependent on them for your very natural and spiritual life. Apparently that is what has happened with many victims of abuse; they have given up their lives to maltreatment and manipulation. You are going to be faced with trials in your life and the only way to overcome them and be victorious is with the help of Jesus Christ.

Again, while living on this earth you are going to be faced with troubles from without (situations, people, circumstances, etc.) and from within your own thoughts in your heart, which according to the Word of God is deceitful. The Lord is saying the heart (emotions) and the mind (intellect) are deceitful without His intervention. The mind will have you thinking evil thoughts for no apparent reason, and the heart is unreliable (Jeremiah 17:9,10). Give your thoughts to God and ask Him about such and such. Here is plain old wisdom; when you meet a new man/woman bring them before the Lord and get the Lord's opinion of them, and then follow His directives.

Sharing From My Experiences

I don't know the type of problem(s) you may be facing in life right now, but I can share with you how prayer and encouragement helped me out of a potential volatile situation.

My husband was a compulsive/pathological gambler, and when he won things were fine, but when he lost things were bad. One night after gambling and losing, he was angry. And I became the object of his frustrations. I knew from the sound of his voice this would be another one of *those* nights, I had become tired of those verbal/and or physical fights; moreover, I was a new Christian and renewing my mind by the Word of God. Therefore, I had to encourage myself in the Lord knowing that no matter how big the problem looked, God is always bigger. I prayed silently as I prepared his dinner; "Lord what to do, you see what's going on here. Lord God I don't want to fight tonight. Show me how to handle this situation."

Luke talked about how he wanted to win money for me (the victim is always the excuse, the problem or whatever). I didn't say too much because it didn't matter what I said or didn't say, in his state of mind there would be a verbal confrontation if the Lord didn't intervene.

But I was encouraging myself in the Lord trusting Him to work in the situation, but not knowing how He would work. Luke ate his dinner and asked for a beer. I gave him the beer, he sat in his easy chair drinking his beers, and I finished cleaning the kitchen while praying silently. Finally he said he was going to take a nap and would be up in half an hour. That half an hour turned into twenty-four hours. When he got up the next evening he asked joking, "Honey what was in those beers?" That was just one of the many situations that the Lord worked on my behalf when I encouraged myself in Him and prayed.

The Word tells us "Be careful for nothing; but in every thing by prayer and supplications with thanksgiving let your request be made known unto God. And the peace of God which passeth all understanding, shall keep hearts and minds through Christ Jesus." Philippians 4:6,7.

> *The above scenario was on the lighter side. The following is darker and more sinister.*

On another occasion my husband and I got into an argument and it ended in me almost losing my life. I will not go into lengthy details I'll be brief and to the point giving the necessary facts. On this particular evening my husband came home with two of this truck driver friends. The friends waited for him to get dressed to go out for the evening. In the bedroom we started talking about money and I didn't want him to take the bill money to gamble it all away. The talk escalated into an argument, and the argument into a fight. Now we had fought before, but this one was demonic in nature. I don't know who passed the first blow, but the next thing I knew I was on the floor being dragged down the hallway which led into the living room area. What were the two friends doing? Good questions. They sat mesmerized like zombies in the living room. From the living room area there was a clear view of the hallway leading to the other rooms. While my husband beat me in the hallway right in clear view of them they never uttered a word in protest. They sat as if paralyzed, frozen in time. Then my husband put me in a choke hold and I couldn't move. He kept saying that he was gong to kill me. In all of our fights he never mentioned *killing*, but this time was different. It was something in his voice that was not himself. Believing that he would kill me I struggled all the more to get loose. But then I heard the voice of the Holy Spirit intervening "G*o limp, do not struggle. Go limp, stop moving.*" I didn't understand, but I obeyed and stopped struggling and let my body go completely limp. When he let me go he moved away, leaving me lying there, and went into the living room. His friends no longer mesmerized got their hats and they all left. For the next few days I was prompted by the Holy Spirit to pray in the spirit (in other tongues). It was during that time that I finally made up my mind to file for a divorce. It didn't matter how much he apologized or what he did, I knew he had snapped that day and I didn't want to experience anything like that again. He had gone too far. I prayed and asked the Lord to lead and guide me in what to do and how to handle the situation. Within one month of him trying to kill me, he was dead! He was a victim of a drive-by shooting.

Are you in a domestic relationship from hell? Did the charming, charisma, magnetic and handsome man you married turn into an evil hateful, pain-inflicting troll from hell? Then encourage yourself in the Lord, pray, and talk with the Father about the situation. Open yourself up to the Lord, tell him if you made a mistake in marrying your spouse, and ask for His help.
I testify, and I do declare, that He is a *situational* God! That means God will work in your affairs, and come to your rescue whenever the situation calls for it. The Lord already knows about the condition but He wants to hear it from you, your mouth, and your point of view. Be honest with the Lord, and if you made a mistake in getting into this relationship talk to Him about it, and ask the Lord to work things for you.

Now the caution, the warning is, you can not dictate to the Lord in how to work things out for you. But trust that He will, accept His ways; and most importantly do whatever He tells you to do while He is working things out for you. Sometimes the things He tells you to do may sound strange, or unorthodox by our standards, because the Lord's ways are not our ways consider "For my thoughts are not your thoughts, neither are your ways my ways, saith the Lord. For as the heavens are higher than the earth, so are my ways higher than your ways, and my thoughts than your thoughts." Isaiah 55:8,9. The Lord will always work and it will be the best for all concerned.

Encouragement: Faith in God the Father.

Faith, trust, belief in God is a principle that will work like the principle of tithing, or the laws of gravity, it's a law, a rule, and anyone can prosper by it. Faith or trust in God is the means by which He will work with you. *Aman* is an Aramaic word means to trust or to believe in, to be faithful, to be sure, believe. Faith means steadiness, steadfastness, faithfulness, trust, honest. It has the idea of faithfulness or certainty. It is especially important in expressing God's faithfulness ". . . But the just shall live by his faith." Habakkuk 2:4.

According to the Bible "Now faith is the substance of things hoped for, the evidence of things not seen." Hebrews 11:1. Faith works in our lives as substance (reality, manifestation, physical material) of things we are hoping to receive. The word faith is Hupostasi in Greek. It means to be placed or stand under, used as a basis or foundation; subsistence, existence, applied to the mind, a firm confidence, constancy (II Corinthians 9:4; 11:17; Hebrews 4:17). Hebrew-Greek Study Bible. (HGSB).

According to the dictionary substance means something that has mass and occupies space, matter, material constitution. The ultimate reality that underlies all manifestation, physical material . . . which has discrete existence. Webster Ninth New Collegiate Dictionary.

Just because we can't see a thing does not mean it does not exist. It exist but in another realm, another dimension we can't apprehend until it is brought into our existence.

Faith in God, the Originator of all Things

Your situation may have you so depressed in your soul that you faith is very low. However, once you start to study the Word of God, and pray seeking His face then your trust in Him will start to grow. It's all about a personal relationship with the Lord. Your faith should be in God not in things, or in people per se. With faith in God you believe that God will manifest the things that you are hoping for. Therefore, faith and praying go hand in hand. ". . . I say unto you, what things so ever ye desire, when ye pray, *believe* that ye receive them and ye shall have them." Mark 11:24. Faith is active and alive, and it's always moving taking us higher in Christ Jesus.

The main idea is that you trust God in all things, "But without faith it is *impossible* to please him [God] for he that cometh to God must believe that he is, and that he is a rewarder of them that diligently seek him." Hebrews 11:6.

I believe that we either have missed a very important aspect of God, or have not tried to learn of His ways. But God does not speak just to speak. When He speaks His Words are spirit and life. When God speaks, men live and men die. He speaks things into existence. He has spoken from the foundation of the world the things that He has for you. You see, you are just beginning to receive what He has spoken in your life before you were born. This is your time to received what He has for you. God is very precise, exact, accurate and specific. God knows the number of stars in the galaxy. You see the Lord has placed the moon is so far from the earth. And if the sun were any closer we would burn up, if any farther we would freeze. God knows the number of hairs on your head. In essence He has your life figured out from beginning to end. And He has a plan for your life and it does not include continued abuse.

It is time to arise to His higher standards for you. It is time to elevate and renew/transform your mind to the things He has for you. You may not see yourself as anything but a victim, you may have lived as a victim for many years. But it is time to come out of your victim mentality

What may seem impossible to you is very possible to God. What seems incredible or impossible for you to do is very credible and possible for God to do in you and through you. The strength you do not have, He has for you. He is waiting for you to agree with Him for your life. It is time to cut the apron strings of generational abuse. Abuse may have been passed on to you, yet, you do not have to pass it on any further. It is time to use the cure—your God given intellect/mind to get out of you abusive situation. Consider God's encouragement, "The Lord is with thee, thou mighty man of valour." Judges 6:12. "And the Lord said unto him, Surely I will be with thee . . ." vs. 16. God is the same yesterday, today and forever. What He has done for one He will do for you_ only believe.

When God speaks it is so_ things happen when He speaks into your life. God made man, the earth, and everything in it by His Word, "For ever, O Lord, thy word is settled in heaven." Psalm 119:89, "So shall my word be that goeth forth out of my mouth; it shall not return unto me void; but it shall accomplish that which I please, and it shall prosper in the thing whereto I sent it." Isaiah 55:11.

How many times have you said that you would leave your abuser and how many times have you actually left, and returned. What happened? Your words didn't have the power to carry out your convictions. There used to be a time when a person spoke a word and it was his bond. He was bound by his word to keep it.

When the Lord God speaks a thing He has the power to fulfill what He has spoken. And He is bound by His Word to fulfill it. You see when the Lord gives you a word it is of great benefit to all concerned to take heed to it. The Lord and His ways are so loving and His words so powerful that he can end a relationship amicably. The question is, will you seek Him and have faith in His words and ways for you? Remember faith acts, and has movement.

Faith without works, without putting action to what you believe is dead. (James 2:17). Many folks may say that they have faith, and it may be true. But the question is who is the faith in? Is it in themselves, material goods, people, in their own abilities, socio/

economic status, or is it in God? God the Father wants your heart, and mind to come into agreement with His heart.

Therefore, if you want to recover your life and learn to do things God's way then you must renew your mind by the Word of God. You have tried it your way, you have tried it their way, you have tried the system's way, now try it God's way. That means you must really want in your spirit and soul to change and have a new way of life from God's perspective.

When your faith is in God He is always working on your behalf. He is the real mover and shaker in your world: you are the helper, put another way, He is the Power that's influencing you. "And this is the confidence that we have in him, that, if we ask anything according to his will, he heareth us; And if we know that he heareth us, whatsoever we ask, we know that we have the petitions that we desired of him." I John 5:14 15.

The Bible was given for the specific purpose of revealing God's will for us; that is how to conduct ourselves with Him and our relationships with others. Whatever we need is in the Word of God for us. (Torry 1971) states, "So when I go to God and ask for wisdom, if I believe [in] the name of the Son of God, I Know with absolute certainty that God has heard my prayer and that wisdom will be granted".

❖ *It is not the Lord's will His desire, that you should be in bondage to no man. We are all free in Christ Jesus. What is your will?*

Putting Your Hand to the Plow

Like a farmer working hard to plow his field. We must plow/ cultivate our spiritual life by turning over the Word of God to see what He has for us.

Below is a short list of promises in the Bible that may help you in praying your needs out to the God the Father. Pray your needs, what you want the Lord to do in your life. Then write out what you plan to do yourself. Remember, faith without doing something to bring it about is dead (James 2:17). God the Father is not going to do what He has empowered you to do.

On the following pages are short exercises to complete using the Word of God.
If you don't see your favorite scripture add it and pray it back to God the Father, through Jesus Christ His Son.

- Salvation—Romans 10:9, 10
- Marital problems—Eph.5:21-33, 4:31,32; Pet. 3:1-7; Rom. 13:10; Ps. 101:2; I Pet. 3:8-11; Prov. 3:5,6, 10:12; I Pet 1:22.
- Peace—Isa. 26:3; Eph. 2:13, 14; Philippians 4:6, 7; Psalm 4:8, 29:11
  Forgiveness-II Cor. 5:17; I John 1:9, Colo. 3:13
  Fellowship with Jesus—John 15:4, 5, 7
- Guardian—II Thess 3:3; Psalm 3:3; 61:3
- Sufficiency—Philippians 4:13
- Financial troubles: Ps. 32:1;Lk. 6:38; I Cor. 16:2; II Cor. 9:6-8;Mal. 3:10-12; Mt. 6:31-33; Phil.4:19.; Ps. 34:10
- When troubles come-II Cor. 4:8, 9, John 14:1; Isa. 43:2; I Pet. 5:7
- Physical illness—I Pet. 2:24; Ps. 103:3; Isa. 53:5, Jere. 17:14, 30:17a

- Holy Spirit-I Cor. 6:19; Romans 5:5; John 7:38, 39, 16:7, 13; Acts 1:4, 5, 8; Acts 2:4.
- Salvation—Romans 3:23, 6:23; 5:8; 10:8-10.
- Faith—Heb. 1:1; 11:6, 12:2; Mark 11:22-24; II Cor. 5:7
- Fearful-II Tim. 1:7; Romans 8:15; I John 4:18; Ps. 81:1-4; Prov 3:25, 26; Ps. 56:11; Jn.14:27; Ps. 27:1,3. Heb. 13:6.
- Strength-Daniel 10:19; Ps. 119:28; Isa. 30, 40:31; 15; Eph. 3:16, 17; Col. 1:10-12.

Example:

Father God (pray your need). Father, I need affordable housing for my family, help me to find it (give particulars). In Jesus' name. Amen.

What will be your hands-on application? Start looking for affordable housing, with the particulars you asked the Lord for.

_____

_____

Lord (pray your need) have faith it will be done.

_____

_____

_____

_____

_____

_____

What will be your hands-on application?

_____

_____

_____

_____

_____

_____

Lord (pray your need)

_____

_____

_____

_____

_____

What will be your hands—on application?

_____

_____

_____

_____

_____

Lord (pray your need)

_____

_____

_____

_____

_____

What will be your hands—on application?

_____

_____

_____

_____

_____

*"Be strong, confident and of good courage . . . Only you
be very courage . . ." Joshua 1:6,7. Amplified Bible.*

Empowerment: In the Word

The definition of empower from the dictionary: "to give
official authority or legal power". Webster's Dictionary.

The word p*ower* comes from the Aramaic is Y'ad. It means
ability, hand, power, assistance, physical hand, which may be good
or evil. Power or empower is also called exousia-right (Acts 26:12);
dunamis-strength (Matthew 9:8;Luke 4:3), and Kratis dominion(Jude
25).

God empowered Adam and Eve and gave them free will the
ability to make decisions, whether right or wrong, but cautioned to
obey (Genesis 2:17). Our first parents made the decision to disobey
their creator. They listened, and yielded to the temptation of the
enemy/Satan that challenged God's Word. Our first parents by their
disobedience turned the whole human race upside down, for all
disobedience is sin. Their seed would reproduce, and populate the
earth, reproducing sin into the world. "For all have sinned and come
short of the glory of God." (Romans 3:23).

Since we are of the same human race, the same gene pool,
so to speak, we have reproduced sin in the world and the cycle
continues. But God had a plan and in the fullness of time God sent
His only begotten Son Jesus into the world to die to atone for our
sin, past, present and future; for without the shedding of blood there
is no remission of sin (Heb. 9:22).

By the Word God created heavens and earth, and by His
word they will be dissolved. The same principle applies to your life.
Who God says you are you are, but you must come into agreement
of what He has spoken about you. There are many reasons for a
woman to stay with an abuser as discussed earlier. However, a
person may also have a low opinion of themselves and have come
to agree with what an abuser has said about them. "Death and life
are in the power of the tongue: and they that love it shall eat the fruit

thereof." Proverbs 18:21. Are you slowly dying by eating the fruit of death which comes from your abuser's mouth?

Allow me to digress for a moment. I feel the Holy Spirit is saying that some of you are spiritually killing your children with negative, unproductive words that tear down their self esteem. Speak life to your children, especially those coming from abusive families. It is vitally important to help to build up these young people who have seen, and experienced more than they should have in their young lives. It's significant for them to know that although they might have come from abusive families they do not have to perpetuate the violence in their lives on to others. Teach them that there's another way to handle life's adversities. Could it be that some of our children who are bullies in school have come from domestic violent homes and are modeling that same dysfunctional behavior? This is something to think about. When abusive behaviors occur in the home, it do not stay in the home. The negative behaviors travel out into the community and to others. So, speak life to your children. "A wholesome tongue is a tree of life." Proverbs, 15:4.

Okay, back to encouragement. It is God's perspective of who you are which makes the difference and that's where you must bridge the gap; between what God thinks of you, and what you think of yourself. Accept His life_ giving words and live. We sometimes see our self-worth in view of what others think of us. However, if you would allow God's perspective of you to determine who you are then He will present the real you and the plans He has for you "For I know the thoughts that I think toward you, saith the Lord, thoughts of peace, and not of evil, to give you an expected end." Jeremiah 29:11. It is all about God's view of you, His plans for you and thus His validation of you.

There are many self-help books on the market to build up your self-esteem on being a better you. I am not trying to build your flesh or flatter your ego, the carnal man in you. What I am endeavoring to do is to give you a healthy, perspective of who God says you are in Him. To help empower you by His Word which says that you can be renewed in the spirit of your mind; and to be what He has ordained for you. Once your spirit is built up you will have a better view of who you are in Christ. God always sees us from His perspective which is the correct one. And if you are willing, and obedient, with the Lord's help you can do great exploits, and accomplish great things for His kingdom.

Empowerment includes some of the following:

> ➢ the power to make your own decisions
> ➢ the power to exercise assertiveness
> ➢ the power to change for the better
> ➢ the power to admit your short coming
> ➢ the power to overcome your short comings

"Our chief want is someone who will inspire us to be what we know we could be." Emerson

According to (Gruen 2000), "self-confidence, then can also mean being self-ware, feeling at home with yourself in your own skin independently of anyone else."

Empower Yourself:
Studying and Practicing the Word

You become empowered by the Word of God. You learn the Word of God, and become empowered by reading His Word. I've heard battered women say that their Christian husband use the Word of God against them. You must search the scriptures for yourself to see what the Lord is saying to you. You must learn the Word for yourself and then apply the word of God to your life and your situations. You replace worldly ideas, the old nature with the Word of God which gives you God's perspective, thus renewing your mind. You must be like the Bereans "These were nobler than those in Thessalonica, in that they received the word with all readiness of mind, and searched the scriptures daily, whether those things were so." Acts 17:11.

According to one Bible teacher Adrian Rodgers, whenever you study the Bible ask yourself three questions: 1) What did it mean at that time? 2) What does it mean now, today? and 3) What does it mean to me personally? God is a personal God and desires to speak directly to you about your present situation and give you strategies to help you. But you have a responsibility to seek the Lord and obey what He tells you to do.

The Lord Jesus wants to empower you in the Word. This is what the Bible says to us all.

- ". . . stand and see this great thing which the Lord will do before your eyes . . ." I Sam. 12:16.
- "The things which are impossible with men are possible with God. "Lk. 18:27.
- "God is not a man that He should lie. Has He said, and will He not do it?" Num. 23:19.
- "But let patience have its perfect work, that you may be perfect and complete, lacking nothing." Js. 1:4.
- "If God be for us, who can be against us?" Rom. 8:31.

- ". . . be strong in the grace that is in Christ Jesus." II. Tim. 2:1.
- "But now ye also put off all these: anger, wrath, malice, blasphemy, filthy communication out of your mouth." Col. 3:8.
- "Set your mind on things above, not on things on the earth." Col. 3:2.
- "Whatever you do, do it heartily, as to the Lord and not to men, . . ." Col. 3:23.
- "If you can believe, all things are possible to him who believes." Mk. 9:23.
- "Be strong and of good courage; do not be afraid, nor be dismayed, for the Lord your God is with you wherever you go." Josh. 1:9.
- "And has He not given you rest on every side?" I Chr. 22:18.
- "You will not need to fight this battle. Position yourselves, stand still and see the salvation of the Lord, who is with you, . . ." II Chr. 20:17.
- "In the world you will have tribulation; but be of good cheer, I have overcome the world." Jn. 16:33.
- ". . . consider that the sufferings of this present time are not worthy to be compared with the glory which shall be revealed in us." Rom. 8:18.
- "Yet in all these things, we are more than conquerors through Him who loved us." Rom. 8:37.
- "Nothing can separate us from the love of God which is in Christ Jesus our Lord." Rom. 8:39.
- "And we know that all things work together for good to those who love God, to those who are the called according to His purpose." Rom. 8:38.
- ". . . be watchful in all things, endure afflictions, do the work of an evangelist, fulfill your ministry." II Tim. 4:5.
- "Fight the good fight, finish the race, and keep the faith." II. Tim. 4:7.(paraphrased)
- "I can do all things through Christ who strengthens me." Phil 4:13.
- "(You) have overcome them, because He who is in you is greater than he that is in the world." I Jn. 4:4.

- "Being confident of this very thing, that He who has begun a good work in you will complete it until the day of Jesus Christ, . . ." Phil 1:6.
- "Rejoice in the Lord always. Again I say, rejoice!" Phil 4:4.
- Let no corrupt communication proceed out of your mouth . . . Eph.4:29.
- ". . . Be ye kind one to another, tender-hearted, forgiving . . . even as God for Christ's sake hath forgiven you." Eph. 4:32.
- Do not answer a fool according to his folly, Lest you also be like him. Prov.25:4.

Now, with prayerful meditation using the scriptures above, write out what you think the Lord is speaking to you about your situation(s). Use as many scriptures as needed, and note scripture reference(s).

Example: *Due to a pattern of verbal abuse from my spouse I choose not to retaliate in like manner when he cussed(cursed) me. I put anger, wrath, malice, and cussing(cursing) words out of my mouth. Colossians 3:8. And I will not let corrupt words come out of my mouth to belittle him (Eph. 4:29).*

You do not have to use what I've written below, you can write your own personal scenarios. But use appropriate bible scriptures to back up what you have said.

I know I started the fight last night I am taking responsibility

_____

_____

_____

_____

_____

_____

_____

_____

If your spouse walked out on you today, after the initial shock, what do you think would be your feelings, and your course of action?

_____
_____
_____
_____
_____
_____
_____
_____
_____
_____

If you are in a volatile relationship and your spouse or intimate partner left you do you believe God had a hand in it? State your rationale.

_____
_____
_____
_____
_____
_____
_____
_____

If your partner left (for good) would you initially try to get your partner back, or would you praise the Lord and use their closet space to expand your wardrobe? Be honest with yourself.

_____
_____
_____
_____
_____
_____
_____
_____

I didn't feel intimidated when my spouse threatened me because:

_____
_____
_____
_____
_____
_____
_____
_____
_____

I am unemployed and my spouse has left us (children) with no financial means.

_____
_____
_____
_____
_____
_____
_____
_____

I have to admit that I've been comfortable in my situation, but now I want to change.

_____
_____
_____
_____
_____
_____
_____
_____

When my spouse refused to pay the rent and buy food I knew that God would provide. Or I did not know what to do, or where to turn for support.

_____

_____

_____

_____

_____

_____

_____

_____

_____

My partner said if I didn't do such and such that he would fix me good.

_____

_____

_____

_____

_____

_____

_____

_____

_____

❖ *If you want your mind renewed you must be born again.*
 "Marvel not that I said unto thee, Ye must be born again."
 John 3:7

The Word

There are many ways that a person can gain power, ability, and courage to do what must be done in an abusive relationship; however, the most effective and lasting ways are through the Word of God. Remember, a principle is a law or rule, something that is unchangeable, that will work as long as the person works it. The word for renew is *Ananeoo*, it means to make young again, to be renewed insofar as spiritual vitality is concerned. It is qualitatively new. Therefore in order for our minds to be renewed we must allow it to be renewed by being regenerated by the washing of the Word of God. ". . . But according to his mercy he saved us, by the washing of the regeneration, and renewing by the Holy Ghost." Titus 3:5b. The principle, the rule, is that we are saved by God's grace through faith in Jesus Christ, and our minds can only be renewed by the Word of God. It's a divine principle that God put in effect so that our minds can be renewed.

We can also use the word transform in connection with renewing the mind. "And be not conformed to this world: but be ye transformed by the renewing of your mind . . ." Romans 12:2. The word transform is a Hebrew word *Yatsar*, pronounced *yaw-tsar*, which means to press, narrow, to be straightened through squeezing into shape, determined to frame the mind. Hebrew-Chaldee Dictionary (HGSB).

There was a toy on the market in the 70's or 80's called the Transformers it advertised as transforming itself from a jeep to a robot without taking it apart. It was interesting to see how it was maneuvered to changed modes. If it was in jeep mode you could twist the head one way, and the body frame, legs and arms another way until you positioned it into a robot; all without disassembling the unit.

That's the picture of being transformed, by the renewing of our minds by the Word of God. We must push out the old way of thinking and s q u e e z e in the Word of God daily, thus transforming the old way of thinking, and talking to the new way of life in Christ.

You are God's handiwork created in Christ Jesus for good works, and your works your ideas, thoughts and inspirations start in your mind, and manifest themselves outwardly in your body. Therefore your mind must be pleasing to the Lord. And you can be renewed in our mind if you will adhere to God's rule of: prayer, studying the Word, worship and fasting.

In like manner of a farmer who plants seeds in the ground. He expects a good harvest, but that expectation is not without hard work. And like a farmer who plants seeds we are able to plant the Word of God in our hearts. And like the farmer who pulls up weeds we too are able to pull up and refuse evil thoughts and deeds in the body.

The farmer irrigates his plants; we too are able to wash ourselves daily in the Word of God. He uses insecticide; like so, we too are to kill everything that is not like the Word of God in our lives. The farmer covers the seeds in adverse weather; we are able to cover ourselves with the blood of Jesus at all times. And when the time to harvest the crop comes the farmer can be assured that he has done all that he could to yield a good harvest. Likewise, when we do all that the Lord God requires of us the Lord will actually renew the mind, so you can bring forth a good harvest.

Again, like farming, renewing your mind is a hands-on approach. You can't plant seeds in the ground and expect that all is well without any intervention on your part. Equally you must practice intervening in your thought-life daily. Most importantly practice those things that the Lord is speaking to you for a transformed mind. Here's the caveat, you are going to mess up every once in a while just because you are human. But the Lord knows that you will fall so He is there to help you. The Bible tells us that a just man falls seven times, but the Lord will pick him up (Proverbs 24:16). And after consistently living your life in the Word things will get better, and after a while you will be living a victorious holy life in Christ Jesus.

It is God's desires that we are transformed in our minds by the power of His Word. God the Father knew that we would fall from grace; so from the foundation of the world He put in what I call the *redemptive clause* to redeem us back to Himself. "And I will put enmity between thee and the woman, and between thy seed and her seed; it shall bruise thy head, and thou shalt bruise his heel." Genesis 3:15. Therefore in the fullness of time God sent His Son Jesus into the world to redeem fallen man and restore man to his rightful place in God (John 1:3, 4).

God the Son atoned for the sins of the world by his death on the cross. If you put your trust in Jesus Christ, your sins, past, present and future have been atoned or covered; and when you die, you will go to heaven. Your spirit man is saved, that's the part of you that will live forever with a renewed body. Therefore, we must work with Him for the renewing, the regeneration of our minds. The word regeneration is *paliggenesis,* it means a recovery, renovations, a new birth, to become new again, regeneration of the soul. Lexical Aid to the New Testament (HGSB).

Jesus Christ who died for us wants us whole, holy and walking in fellowship with Him. "Can two walk together, except they be agreed?" Amos 3:3. That's like two people who agree to walk to the park together, but can't agree on the best route to take. They are divided on the simple issue of directions and they stand debating the best route; something has to give if they intend to walk together. The same is with our relationship with God, "If we say that we have fellowship with him, and walk in darkness, we lie and do not tell the truth." I John 1:6. Our heavenly Father wants us to agree with what He's saying about our lives, and enjoy fellowship with Him.

How can we have fellowship with Christ when we are living in darkness working the works of the enemy? If we are not following Christ closely, adhering to His Word and His life, then we can be just like Judas Iscariot working our own agendas in the name of Christ, thus, not really converted at all. You see the Lord Jesus give us all time (in the vernacular) *to clean up our act* to renew our minds by His Word which is able to cleanse us from all unrighteousness. But there are many who are still allowing the enemy to use their minds as if they were never converted to Christ.

There are many who name the name of Christ who are still abusing verbally, physically sexually, and emotionally. That's just it; the Lord wants to change the minds of His people, ". . . And let everyone that nameth the name of Christ depart from iniquity." II Timothy 2:19b. God the Father does not want His children living a defeated life at the whims of the enemy; but to know that there's hope and they can be transformed in the spirit of their minds.

Pulling Down Strongholds in the Mind

Earlier in the book I talked about *pulling down strongholds.* "Casting down imaginations, and every high thing that exalteth itself against the knowledge of God, and bringing into captivity every thought to the obedience of Christ." II Corinthians 10:5.

If we are going to change our behavior, our way of life, we must change the way we think. And we make our decisions based upon the world around us and our beliefs. That's not a bad thing, God made us thinking human being. However, most often we fail to bring the Word of God into the equation.

Eve the first woman had a perfect mind, and undoubtedly she thought what it would be like to eat of the forbidden tree, and she followed her thought life to death! There was no sin in the world, no corruption, no evil, because God made everything perfect, thus she was perfect and as near to God as anyone could be. But when Satan came to tempt Eve she didn't call on God or even consult her husband. With her thinking process thoroughly intact she made the decision to go against the Word of God. And her lack of obedience caused sin to enter into the world, for all disobedience is sin.

When we come up against situations, circumstances, obstacles, or unforeseen events, we must learn to seek the Lord on how to handle the problem. Ask His advice about it and how to proceed. Yes, you may already know what to do, but it won't hurt to ask the *All—Knowing, All-Present*, and *All-Powerful One* about it also; it gives you a divine perspective, and in most cases help.

The same goes for our friendships, and love relationships. When you meet a new person, you form an opinion about that person based on most often faulty impressions. You look on the outside, but the Lord sees the heart of a person. There are many women who have made the same mistake in choosing a mate over and over again. Why? Because their data the information they have stored in their minds, has not changed over time. If it has changed it, was not according to the Word of God; therefore, the results are the same. Some women are so happy to be out of the *frying pan* that they jump right into the *skillet!* (See section on Abusers' Traits, Characteristics and Behaviors).

Now that you are learning to renew your mind by the Word of God you can actually take your thoughts captive, to see what God has to say about them, thereby pulling down the strongholds, the negative thoughts, and replacing them with the thoughts of God.

Again we are casting down evil imagination_ rebellious ideas, hatred, jealousies, wrath, envy, negative attitudes, pride, and evil thoughts. And bringing into captivity all thoughts that are against the Word of God. The Word tells us to be: peaceful, longsuffering, kind, gentle, to have self-control, to put away anger, and evil speaking. Let no curse words come out of our mouths (Galatians 5:22; Ephesians 4:29, 31, 32).

Exercise
Pulling Down Strongholds

Below are scenarios where you have the ability to be guided by your own impressions based upon what you are experiencing, or to be guided by the Word of God, thus taking captive evil thoughts. Choose one, or two, and give the rationale for your answers.

First scenario: You are driving the normal speed limit when someone speeding crosses over in your lane abruptly; however, you both come to the red light at the same time.

What do you do? (a) Give him/her a piece of your mind, or (b) Compose yourself and whisper a prayer (c) Look straight ahead not acknowledging his/her erratic behavior.

Rationale. _____
_____
_____
_____
_____

Second scenario: You and your husband have been planning and saving for months to purchased new furniture for your house: dining room and living room furniture. The family has enjoyed the new furniture for about a month. One day you come home from work and all the new furniture is gone. What do you do first? (a) Call the police_ apparently you have been robbed; (b) Call your family for consolation; or (c) Call on God the Father and pray.

Rationale. _____
_____
_____
_____
_____

However, upon further inspection of the house you notice your husband's favorite cap lying on the kitchen counter. He had it on when he left in the morning. You instantly know this is the work of your husband the gambler. What do you do? (a) Call all his friends and report the malicious deed tying to discredit him among his peers; (b) Ask the Lord how to handle this situation and to keep you from going berserk on him; or (c) Take all his good suits and put them in a tub of water.

Rationale. _____
_____
_____
_____
_____

Third and final scenario: It's Thanksgiving Day and you have guest over for a scrumptious Thanksgiving dinner. The football game is over, your guest are now all fat and full and ready to leave.

You bid them goodbye, but along with the guest your husband says he's going out for a little while. Little did you know that your monthly paycheck went along with him. What do you do? (a) Cry in despair; (b) Get angry with God because He could have stopped him; (c) You call your mother and listen to her wisdom in how to handle the situation.

Rationale. _____

_____

_____

_____

_____

All of these scenarios happened to me. I could have chosen to use my old way of thinking to handle the situation, or I could (which I did) listen to, and allow the Word of God to take captive my thoughts, thus, giving me the victory in each situation. Time does not permit me to elaborate on each scenario but they all worked out much better than I could have ever imagined, because I gave the negative thoughts to the Lord and listened to His solutions.

Practical Hands on Work

This is where you can do some more practical work. We could start with a virtue like love, but let's start with a vice like anger. Sadly to say, that's what most people are today-angry. But living with an angry spirit is not where the Lord would have you live and function in your life. The Bible has much to say about anger, and how to deal with it. "He that is slow to anger is better than the mighty; and he that ruleth his spirit than he that taketh a city." Proverbs 16:32.

Remember you being empowered through
practical application of the Word.

It is the Lord's desire that we use the Word to renew/ transform our minds in Him. Use the scriptures below regarding anger, rage, resentment, bitterness, hatred and forgiveness as you complete the following exercises.

- Let every man be swift to hear . . . James 1:19, 20.
- Be ye angry, and sin not . . ." Eph. 4:26.
- For if ye forgive men their trespasses . . ." Matt. 6:14.
- He that is slow to wrath is of great understanding . . ." Prov. 14:29.
- Be not hasty in thy spirit to be angry" Eccl. 7:9.
- . . . avenge not yourselves . . . Vengeance is mine, I will repay saith the Lord. Romans 12:19-24; Heb. 10:30.
- If thine enemy be hungry, give him bread to eat . . ." Prov. 25:21,22.
- Let all bitterness, and wrath and anger and clamour, and evil speaking, be put away from you . . . Eph. 4:31, 32.
- Cease from anger . . . fret not thyself . . . to do evil. Ps. 37:8.
- Forgive us as we forgive others . . . Matt. 6:12, 14, 15.
- When you pray . . . forgive. Mark 11:25-26.
- Love your enemies, do good . . . Luke 6:35-38.
- Lord how often shall my brother sin . . . and I forgive him? Matt. 18:21-22.
- "Father, forgive them . . . Luke 23:33-34.

According to the Bible what are the Lord's thoughts on those who take unfair advantage of you? And according to the Bible what should you do in return?

_____

_____

_____

_____

_____

_____

What do you want the Lord to do to those whom you feel have taken unfair advantage of you?

_____

_____

_____

_____

_____

_____

Is there anyone in particular, or many people in general whom you are angry with for your present situation?

_____

_____

_____

_____

_____

_____

Are there any government, i.e., county municipalities, hospitals, state or private-agencies, that you are angry with? Or are you angry with God the Father? If so, can you forgive Him?

_____

_____

_____

_____

_____

_____

Are you able to express your feeling about these agencies or organizations? Or express your feeling about God the Father?

_____

_____

_____

_____

_____

_____

Can you express your feelings if you are angry with any of your family members, or friends?

_____

_____

_____

_____

_____

_____

If you are currently in an abusive relationship what is it you want God the Father to do for you right now?

_____

_____

_____

_____

_____

_____

Until the Lord opens a way of escape for you what are you going to do to help yourself? You can refer to the back of the book for *Optional Exercise*.

_____

_____

_____

_____

_____

_____

We are told to forgive others like God has forgiven our trespasses and sins. Jesus received all of our sins in His body on the cross. He expects us to forgive those who hurt us.

Are you willing to give up your right to your pain? That means are you willing to give your pain over to Jesus so He can heal you? If so, what do you need to do to receive the healing?

_____

_____

_____

_____

_____

_____

If you are <u>not</u> ready to give up your pain to Jesus can you explain why not?

_____

_____

_____

_____

_____

_____

Can you honestly pray for your abuser, or your enemies at this time?

_____

_____

_____

_____

_____

_____

Catharsis: Your Experiences

The purpose of catharsis is to cleanse the soul, and the spirit, and most importantly to forgive your abuser for hurting you (Psalm 51:7).

Catharsis by definition: Purification that brings about spiritual renewal or release from tension, elimination of a complex, by bringing it to consciousness and affording it expression. Webster New Collegiate Dictionary.

The qualifying factor in your life is love, so you must let go of all the hate, animosity, and bitterness that's in your heart. It's time to release all the hostilities that you may have bottled up in your heart and spirit because of abuse. In other words, purify your emotions, spill the beans, get it out of your system, and cease the warfare raging in your heart, so you can love. Forgive the perpetrator for all the evil deeds done to you. Nevertheless you can only forgive successfully with the Lord's help. You may speak it out, or write it out, or cry it out, the point is get it out of your system, because it's toxic to your well-being, and in renewing your mind. Catharsis is the start of your spiritual renewal.

I will briefly share a cathartic moment.

The time lapse of my husband's death could have been a year or so, I'm not really sure. But one morning I woke out of a deep sleep screaming, I hate you! I hate you! I hate you!! I startled my self with the offending declaration, because I didn't know where those words were coming from. For days afterwards I pondered the words and even condemned myself for uttering them. Later, however, I received a revelation about my disturbing declaration. I hated my husband for taking his frustration, and anger out on me physically. I hated him for being a compulsive gambler who lost every cent he made. I hated him because he died and left me penniless . . . I hated him because he would never become what he could have been, if he had surrendered his life to the Lord. And I hated him because he lied and said, "Honey, I won't be gone long."

Reality had set in and I had to get it all out of my spirit, soul and mind, the good as well as the bad things. Once my heart was clean, and I had forgiven him, I could officially put the past behind and start my life anew. Whatever your situation this is your cathartic moment. Cry your heart out to the Lord, and remember confession is good for the soul, and a good cry is therapeutic.

Your Cathartic Experience

Domestic Violence Duluth Model

According to the Duluth DVIP intervention model of power and control wheel "Battering is one form of domestic or intimate partner violence. It is characterized by the pattern of actions that an individual uses to intentionally control or dominate his intimate partner. That is why the words 'power an control' are in the center of he wheel. A batterer systematically uses threats, intimidation, and coercion to instill fear in his partner. These behaviors are the spokes of the wheel. Physical and sexual violence holds it all together-this violence is the rim of the wheel" See the Duluth model at the following URL www.theduluthmodel.org/wheelgallery.php

Riding the Cycle of Abuse

If you have read the book, and worked through the exercises you no longer have to cycle through or repeat sequence of violent events in your life. You have the power to stop what you are thinking, thus changing your behavior in any given situation. Remember the mind tells or gives the body information or clues on what, or what not to do.

Definition of cycle. "An interval of time during which a sequence of a reoccurring succession of events or phenomenon is completed: a course of series of events or operations that recur regularly and usually lead back to the starting point: a circular or spiral arrangement . . ." Webster Ninth New Collegiate Dictionary.

Note: *Always keep yourself out of harm's way and get to a place of safety.*

You can write or imagine your own scenario, for the principle of cycling the sequential order of events will be the same, unless an event is changed.

(**A**) Something happens, which causes (**B**) how you think about what has just occurred, and then (**C**) how you respond to that event. You can't help (**A**) from happening, you can't change anyone's behavior, but you can change (**B**) your thinking process, thus changing (**C**) how you respond to the event.

Riding the cycle of abuse looks something like this. A discussion turns ugly, **tension builds,** and an argument ensues. There's an **explosion of anger**: verbal abuse, physical, emotional, and/ or sexual abuse. The person later apologizes. **Honeymoon phase**, blaming his/her behavior on outside circumstances, and the couple then makes up. Things are good for awhile between them until something happens, and the process starts all over again_ new circumstance but same outcome. It's a cycle, a wheel of abuse going around and around. You can stop riding the cycle of abuse by renewing your mind.

Remember something has to change (hopefully in the positive). You can't change anyone but yourself. "A soft answer turns away wrath" Proverbs 15:1. Remember, it takes two people to argue, and you really don't have to have the last word. Become the better person and pray silently. "In the mouth of the foolish is a rod of pride: but the lips of the wise shall preserve them." Proverbs 14:3.

Here's a personal scenario

(A) Event: My husband was going out on the town without me. He knew that I didn't indulge in the alcohol and partying scene anymore, but still there where things that we could do together.

(B) My thinking process: The more he talked, the more upset I became. He was really having fun with me, but I wasn't laughing. Then I heard in my spirit "Help him to get dress to go out." Of course I wanted to rebuke the enemy of my soul. But it was the Lord speaking. I didn't understand the rationale, but I obeyed.

(C) My response to event. I told my husband that if he was going out flirting then he needed to look good. So I got his favorite clothes and helped him to get dressed.

What changed? (B) My mind, the way I saw things (God's intervention) which changed the whole dynamics of the evening. Of course that was light, and I know all too well that if you are in a volatile situation things are not that simple. Believe me I've been in some very dire situations, one of which I've shared with you in this book. However, allow the Word of God to transform/renew your mind so you will not have to continue to ride the cycle, the wheel of abuse.

Abusers' Traits, Characteristics, and Behaviors

The first instance of abuse was in the Bible when Cain killed his brother Abel out of jealousy.

"Now Cain said . . . let's go out to the field." And while they were in the field, Cain attacked his brother Able, and killed him. Genesis 4:8.

An abuser can be anyone, as evidenced from the Bible. Abusers are in every culture, ethnic group and nationality in the world. There are both male and female abusers, but most perpetrator of abuse are males.

As I mentioned earlier, I was a victim of emotional and physical abuse. And from my experience, I have discovered some characteristics of my former husbands.

Charismatic

They are charismatic/charming. There's a certain attractive quality about them. They are extremely polite, well-mannered, courteous, outwardly respectful, and even delightful to be around. One would say "He's a charmer or Mr. Personality".

Most often they are physically attractive. That's what wins most women over, the smart, handsome type. Most women don't gravitate to men that are not physically appealing to them.

However, there are some abusers who are not so attractive, but there's a quality about them that's appealing that wins the woman over, perhaps he's financially stable.

Most people can't believe that the person is an abuser, because they can't see beyond his/her fascinating personality. In fact in some instances, children, even though they may actually see the abuse, believe that somehow you the victim were the cause of the abuse. Why else would such a sweet person do what he/she does? They don't understand about power and control.

We normally look at the outward appearance of a person, but the Lord looks at the heart of a person (I Samuel 16:7).

Jealousy

An abuser can be extremely hateful and jealous of his/her lover relationships. Usually they have an unhealthy, unfounded suspicion of their spouse/or friend. They can be excessively jealous. In the beginning of a relationship, an abuser may claim that jealousy is a sign of his or her love, however, that type of jealousy has nothing to do with love.

There's a righteous type of jealousy. "You shall not bow down to them (idols) or worship them: for I the lord your God, am a jealous God . . ." Exodus 20:5. And there's an un-righteous type of jealousy "For love is as strong as death, its jealousy un-yielding as the grave." Song of Songs 8:6b.

Controlling

Most abusers whether male of female can be controlling in their behaviors. They must have the upper hand, dominance, and rule in their affairs with their loved ones. One of my husbands tried to control my money and would often steal from my purse if I left it unattended. If they are the chief bread winner they have a tendency to keep all the money. Or if they allow you a small amount they want an account of all that was spent and where.

God is the only One who as power over His creations. "He rule forever by His power, His eyes watch the nations-let not the rebellious rise up against Him." Psalm 66:7.

Deceptive

Most abusers can be very deceptive, misleading, illusory, dishonest, and full of guile. They somehow manage to juggle situations, people and circumstance to their benefit. They are convincing impostors.

". . . Bloodthirsty and deceitful men will not live out half their days." Psalm 55:23b. "The bread of deceit is sweet to a man but afterwards his mouth . . . filled with gravel." Proverbs 20:17. He that hates pretends with his lips, but stores up deceit within him." Proverbs 26:24.

Pride

Most abusers are proud, arrogant, and egotistical, they have an unrepentant spirit about abuse, and most things for that matter. They believe what they have done was to keep things in control for *your sake*. They may cry, plead, and even ask for your forgiveness, but is not sincere, for soon the slander and abuse starts all over again.

"Whoever slanders his neighbor in secret, him will I put to silence." Psalm 101:5. God hates a "proud look, a lying tongue and hands that shed innocent blood." Proverb 6:17,18.

Stalker

Perpetrators of abuse often track/follow their victims, and stalk out their whereabouts. One of my sister's ex-husbands sneaked around her house peering into her window, and when she came out of the house, he beat her up. An abuser will check their victim's car mileage, monitor phone call, and text messages, or use other social media or other stalking behaviors.

Only the eyes of God the Maker of man has the right to know where man is at all times. *"For the eyes of the Lord run to and fro though out the whole earth to show Himself strong in behalf of those whose hearts are blameless toward Him. 2 Chronicles 16:9.*

Red flag of abusive behaviors include:

- Destroying property
- Threatening behaviors to your and others
- Blaming you for his outbursts
- Poor self-image
- History of family violence
- Being unfaithful in the marital relationship. If they can't control you they will seek to control someone else, because they have a need to be in control at all times.
- Alcohol or drug addiction, or an addiction of some other type. My husband was a compulsive gambler.
- Rushing into relationships
- Dr. Jekyll/Mr. Hyde syndrome
- Blowing up in anger at small incidents.
- Isolating their victims(s); He or she may try to cut them off from social support.
- Insecurity or may seem overly confident to make up for a poor self-esteem.
- Blaming others for their feeling of inadequacy
- Saying things that are intentionally cruel and hurtful in order to degrade and humiliate the victim.
- Being unduly moody and unpredictable with mood swings

You are renewing your mind, so be wise, a abusers will not show all of the above signs, but they will display enough red flags for you to know that something is not right. So, what do you do? Pray and ask the Lord for divine interventions, and to show you how to handle the situation. Ask for divine strategies and a plan of escape if that's what you want.

Sometimes talking about the abuse and asking the person to get help might suffice. But if domestic violence is on-going then you should seek help, and a place of safety for yourself and children.

Your thoughts/concerns/strategies.

Renewing Your Mind
From The Inside Out

You have been given information regarding the Dulute Model. Most professionals us this model or an adaptation of the model when addressing violence in intimate relationships.

My effort is to address the issues from a spiritual perspective: working from the inside out. The Holy Spirit who resides within a believer is able to change the way in which they think about a matter. The Holy Spirit uses the Word of God to change a person from the inside out. " . . . the words that I speak to you they are spirit and life." John 6:63. Remember God's way of communicating is through the spirit of a person. The spirit communicates to the mind/ intellect, and the mind communicates to the body, who in turn acts.

"And I will give unto thee the keys [authority, strength, power] of the kingdom of heaven: and whatsoever thou shall bind on earth shall be bound in heaven: and whatsoever thou shalt loose on earth shall be loosed in heaven." Matthew 16:19. And "Again I say unto you: that if two of you shall agree one earth as touching any thing that they shall ask, it shall be done for them of my Father which is in heaven. For where two or three are gathered together in my name, there am I in the midst of you." Matthew 18:19-20.

Keys/Strategies for Renewing the Mind
Binding and Loosing

From the word of God we have keys which denote authority, right and power to bind and loose (or forbid and permit) things on the earth. These keys of authority and power were given to the Church by Jesus Christ Himself. According to, (Zodhiates 1984). "The teaching here is that those things which are conclusively decided by the King in His kingdom of heaven, having been so decided upon, are emulated by the Church on earth, the Church being the true believers whose testimony is the Rock [Christ] . . . We as believers can never make conclusive decision about things, but can only confirm those decisions which have already been made by the King Himself as conclusive in context of His kingdom both on earth (Believers) and in heaven."

We bind or forbid negative things or behaviors that are trying to come into our lives to destroy us. And we loose or permit the positive or good behaviors into our lives. For instances we could say that we bind fear, fear is a spirit and has torment which is not of God. And we loose or permit courage, nerves, guts, valor, encouragement, and hope into our lives, which is of God. It is binding/forbidding and loosing/permitting of things.

Accordingly for everything that is *bound* there should be a corresponding *loosing* of something in its place. There is a mate a corresponding equal for everything in the universe. Observe the Word, "Seek out of the book of the Lord, and read: not one of these shall fail, none shall want her mate . . ." Isaiah 34:16. The God of the universe is a God of balance and not of imbalance. If you bind something then loose something in its place.

For instance, if an abuser called you "crazy woman" you could say "I bind those words, I do not receive those words (binding negative words which have death), and loose positive ones: "I am a child of God, I have a good mind", therefore loosing the

Word of God, affirming your good mind, etc. Remember you are renewing/transforming your mind by Biblical precepts, not trying to go toe—toe in verbal assault with your abuser, which would be counterproductive to renewing your mind.

Binding and Loosing from the Word of God

The power and control wheel are actions, behaviors used by perpetrators of abuse to dominate, rule and control their victims. On the contrary from the scriptures of binding/forbidding and loosing/permitting are proactive and godly strategies meant to counteract the power and control behaviors of a perpetrator against you.

The following are keys or strategies that a person can use in the plan of recovery while renewing the mind, and thus become free of the spokes of the power and control wheel.

1. *Bind intimidation.* You have the key the power, the authority to **bind, the fear of intimidation, threats, and bullying.** You no longer have to accept the fear of intimidation-like gestures, and abusive language. You now understand that fear brings about torment, but the Word of God brings peace. "I, even I, am he that comforteth you: who art thou, that thou shouldest be afraid of a man that shall die . . ." Isa. 51:12a. "Fear thou not; for I am with thee; be not dismayed; for I am thy God: I will strengthened thee; yea, I will help thee; yea . . ." Isa. 41:10. "Preserve my life from fear of the enemy" Ps. 64:1b. "But whoso hearkeneth unto me shall dwell safely, and shall be quiet from fear of evil.' Prov. 1:33. You bind fear by dwelling in the secret place of the Almighty (Ps. 91:1). You bind fear by putting your trust in the Lord not fearing what man can do to you (Ps. 56:11). But don't stand there while he tries to hit you, use wisdom, and get out of harms way! Bind the spirit of fear and loose faith into your spirit by using your offensive weapon of prayer, praise and worship, and pray against the works of an abuser. Read 2 Chronicles 20:1-25, and see the great things God did for His people. He's the same God today.

2. *Bind emotional abuse.* You have the key to **loose, free up emotional soundness**. You are made in the image of God, with a unique personality, gifts and talents. You are valuable, you have self-worth, self-confidence, and you are complete and whole in Christ. Pray that God will strengthen you with might by His Spirit in the inner—man (Eph. 3:16). "But they that wait upon the Lord shall renew their strength . . ." Isa. 40:31, "He healeth the broken in heart, and bindeth up their wounds." Ps. 147:3. Loose, let loose emotional soundness and free yourself by speaking the words of God out loud to yourself. And use your offensive weapon of prayer every day to better yourself, and your condition.

3. *Bind isolation.* You have the key to **loose, free up interaction with others**. A person no longer has to be isolated, cut off, separate, or detached from family and friends, and un-able to form personal relationship on their own. God has given all people the power to make choices for themselves. Free of domination and mirco—management of an abuser. With a renewed mind you can now say "I can do all things through Christ which strengtheneth me." Phil. 4:13. and ". . . The Lord shall be thy confidence, and shall keep thy foot from being taken." Prov. 3:26.

Your weapon of warfare is always in your mouth, prayer, praise and worship. Speak it OUT and free yourself!

4. *Bind denial and blaming.* You have the key to bind negative thoughts. You are not responsible for your abuser's violent behavior. A perpetrator or an abuser must learn to accept his/her negative behaviors toward others, and the consequences of their actions, instead of blaming others for his action. "Create in me a clean heart, O God; and renew a right spirit within me." Ps. 51:10. Denial of abusive actions is unacceptable for a renewed mind. "For I acknowledge my transgression; and my sin is ever before me." Ps. 51:3. The victim of abuse can **loose,** let go of negative feelings toward an abuser. Go "cathartic" to

the Lord in prayer, spill your guts get it all out of your system, and allow the Lord God to heal and cleanse your soul. Pray for your abuser, pray that the Word of God sinks deep into your spirit and walk in the newness of life, without fear.

5. *Bind the use of children as weapons.* You have the key to **Bind, forbid,** and reject negative use of God's gift children. Children are your future, and a gift from God. Teach a child how to live which does not include abusive behaviors. Prov. 22:6. Children are to be loved and cherished, and not used as pawns or weapons in marital disputes between parents. Remember that children are like little sponges they soak up everything they hear and see, and you are role models to them. What behaviors are they displaying at school or with their peers? Is your child a bully? **Bind** abusive and physical aggression in the presence of your children. Refrain from speaking negative of your spouse in the presence of children. Negative words have a way of coming back to haunt you (Ephesians 4:29). Pray for peace in your spouse, and pray for your children to have a peaceful home environment.

6. *Bind male privilege.* You have the key to l**oose, permit, allow and sanction** loving relationships in your home (Gen. 2:18). God Himself ordained marriage, but **without** violence (Heb. 13:4). Take time with each other, talk of your likes, dislikes, and how you can help each other in your endeavors. Love your spouse (but love yourself also). Men are to love their wives and protect them, as Christ loved the church (Eph. 5:25). Men and women are to work together in unity, and have respect for each other's gifts and talents. God made woman from man's rib, his side, to walk and work side by side; and not from his feet to be trampled on. Be kind to one another and do not pay evil for evil, but overcome evil with good (Prov. 25:21-22; Rom. 12:17-21). Love with the love of God and pray for your spouse daily (Ps. 143:9).

7. *Bind economic abuse.* You have the key to **loose economic stability**. It is God who gives power to get wealth

(Deuteronomy 8:18). And my God shall supply all my need (Phil 4:13.). God tells you to tithe and He will provide for your need (Malachi 3:10-13). You are to seek the Lord your God for your provision (Matthew 6:31-33). Even if you are in an economically abusive relationship God is able to provide for you so you can have what you need. Pray for God to give you witty inventions so that it can be a source of income for the family.

8. *Bind coercion and threats.* You have the key to **loose a non-violent attitude**. With a renewed mind you no longer have to accept verbal threats or coercions into your spirit. The Bible tells us, "Be not hasty in thy spirit to be angry; for anger resteth in the bosom of fools. Eccl. 7:9. With your renewed mind you can admit to and accept any wrong-doings on your behalf and accept the responsibility thereof. With a renewed mind you can refuse participation in illegal activity by coercion or threats or any actions that goes against your renewed conscience. "For men ought to obey God rather than man." Acts 5:29. If anything is going to be changed in your life for the better you must pray, and stand up for what you believe, and God is standing with you.

9. *Loose forgiveness.* You have the key to **loose forgiveness**. Forgiveness is very big with God the Father. For He has forgiven the sin for all those who put their trust in His Son Jesus Christ (Colossians 2:13; Isa. 1:8). With a renewed mind you can forgive your perpetrator "Forbearing one another, and forgiving one another, if any man has a quarrel against you: even as Christ forgave you, so also do ye." Col. 3:13. It is imperative that you forgive and do not harbor, keep or allow ill feeling to set up and take root in your heart. An un-forgiving spirit is toxic to your soul and colors everything you do with others. Confess your faults get things out of your heart that would hold you captive to the spirit of un-forgiveness (I John 1:9). Do not try to get even, but forgive (Romans 12:21). Pray that your heavenly Father will help you to forgive those who have deeply hurt you (Mark 11:25).

10.   *Bind your tongue.* You have the key to **bind/forbid a** verbally abusive tongue. Aggressive, or cruel, language can be more devastating than physical violence. There was a nursery rhyme that said "Sticks and stones can break my bones, but words can never hurt me." That's a fallacy evil malicious words go deep into your spirit and linger there. Only the Word of God can retrieve and take the power away from the words. The tongue can buy more trouble than you are willing to pay for. There's a saying in the vernacular "You tongue will write a check that your behind can't cash (James 3:5, 6,8). You have the ability to allow the Lord to sanctify your tongue with good things to say. Read the Word, and practice speaking good things, and pray that the Lord Jesus will sanctify you wholly in all your behavior.

Attachment Deficits

According to some human behaviorist it is believed that most perpetrators of abuse have what has been called attachment deficits.

(Greif, G 1997). The term *"Attachment Deficits"* refers to the inability to form and maintain viable attachment bonds, because of something that has happened in a person's childhood. "It includes doubts about one's capacity to love, and be loved, to trust, and be trusted, to feel compassion and be worthy of compassion, to maintain interest in a significant other . . . . The evidence seems overwhelming that spouse abusers regardless of sexual orientation, exhibit great difficulties in intimacy, trust, mutuality, compassion, jealousy, fear of abandonment and fear of engulfment, that is fear that the self will diminish or disintegrate in sustained proximity to another.

We live in a cruel world because of sin, thus human nature is not perfect. That is why God tells us that we must be born again. "Jesus answered, I assure you most solemnly I tell you, unless a man is born of water and the Spirit he cannot enter the kingdom of God . . . What is born of flesh is flesh . . . what is born of the Spirit is spirit." John 3:5,6a. Amplified Bible. Whether you are a victim/survivor or a perpetrator of abuse the transformation of your mind can be true and lasting if you choose God's way.

How is the Mind Renewed?

*"The secret things belong unto the Lord our God; but
those things which are revealed belong unto us . . ."*
Deuteronomy 29:29.

How is the mind renewed? I don't know exactly. I do know it's an inside job. I suppose it's like salvation/ conversion to the Lord Jesus Christ, it's a faith thing that can only be accomplished by His Word and the Holy Spirit working with us in the process. And the Lord watches over His Word to perform them in our lives when we believe in Him. He has revealed to us what we are to do with His Word in the natural (the revealed things), and He will complete the process (the secret things). "Forever, O Lord, they word is settled in heaven . . ." Psalms 119:89. So, when the Word of God tells us that our minds can be renewed/transformed and regenerated it can. It is done by practical work: reading and studying the Word, praying and allowing the Word to work in your heart and it will do what it is supposed to do. "What doth it profit my brethren though a man say he hath faith, and have not works? . . . Even so faith, if it hath not works, is dead, being alone. James 2:14, 7.

I dare to say that many who have been abusers have had their minds renewed by the Word of God, and are living a victorious life in Him, the choice is yours.

Most of us wish that we could go back into our past and undo the bad things that happened to us, but we can't. Only God can walk you back into your past heal you of your pain, and bring about healing in your present and future. That's a God thing! However, it does take a walk of faith on your part for the healing to begin. That means that you believe that God will work in your life to bring about healing for the abused as well as the abuser. Your abuser may or may not be willing to renew/transform his/her minds at present. But the Lord wants you to be renewed in your mind so you will not have to continually endure abuse. The Lord God can do great things for you, but if your mind is not being renewed you may go right back into the same type lifestyle.

There are no quick fixes, or escapes in God, this is a walk of faith in Him. God wants to deliver you, but He wants to deliver the spirit of your mind so you will not go back to the same type situation. It's been stated that domestic violence is like an addiction; if it is not cured it will manifest itself in other areas of your life, or in new relationships, and only the Word of God can cure you, because the Word changes who you are.

The Lord God has given you tools from His Word to start the recovery process by renewing your mind through: enlightenment (prayer); encouragement (faith); and empowerment (the Word). If you are willing, and if you sincerely want a renewed mind that will deliver you from a life of abuse then Jesus Christ can help you. Who better to help you than God Himself?

❖ ". . . For I am God, and there is none else; I am God, and there is none like me." Isaiah 46:9b.

Optional Exercise

"Where there is no vision the people perish . . ."
Prov. 29:18.

This is by no means a prerequisite for answered prayers, but a way to keep your faith alive while you are waiting on the Lord for the things He has for you.

You are being renewed by the Word of God working in your life. You no longer have to live a life of abuse. You are becoming healthy and whole in the spirit of your mind. Those things that have been suppressed in your heart and mind are now being brought back to the forefront of your mind as you seek the Lord in prayer, praise and worship. So now is a good time to put actions to your hopes, dreams and desires, and work toward your goals. Write your vision and work on it, because now you can accomplish great things for the Lord.

❧ *I've heard it said if you want to hear God laugh tell Him your plans.*

While you are being renewed in your mind, you are learning how to make better decisions for your life. You weigh the pro and cons. You look at how your decisions will impact your life and the life of your family. You are learning to go before God the Father in prayer talking with Him about your plans, hope, dreams and desires.

The Lord will give us the desires or our hearts after He tweaks them a bit (Ps. 37:4-5). And that's fine because His ways are always the best for us anyway. You are also aware of some of the characteristics of an abuser, you know what to look for before you get into another relationship.

In goal settings and planning some people like to keep things in their minds, that's good if you have the mental capacity and are very focused. Others are visual planners they like to see their goals written somewhere; on their computer, desk in their office, or in their planner. The point is the vision is in front of them to make changes, updates, or deletions as things change. It is a good way of staying on track for the things you want to accomplish in your life.

❖ *"Thy word is a lamp unto my feet and a light unto my path." Ps. 119:105.*

The Word of God is the light for our life, and the Word helps us to live the life that God the Father has for us. And as you read the scriptures, ask the Holy Spirit for understanding He will give us light, to enlighten our path as we travel in this life. For instance there may be things that you want to do. You pray and while reading the word the Holy Spirit may shed light on a particular scripture that will enlighten you on the things your are considering. A little light here, and a little light there, so you won't see the bigger picture and fall back. By the time He sheds light on the path to see the big picture you are already there walking in the vision, that's the wisdom of God.

Write out your short-term goals (five years or less) and your long term goals (ten years or more), the time frame in which you want to see them accomplished, and the outcome of the goals.

Short term goal(s):

_____

_____

_____

_____

_____

Time Frame: _____

Outcome: _____

_____

_____

_____

_____

_____

Activities to accomplish the goal(s)

_____

_____

_____

_____

_____

Long term goal(s):

_____

_____

_____

_____

_____

Time frame: _____

Outcome: _____

_____

_____

_____

_____

_____

Activities to accomplish the goal (s):

_____

_____

_____

_____

Explain if you see the hand of God working with you in your goals.

_____

_____

_____

_____

_____

If you do not see the hand of God working with you, answer these questions.

Are you seeking His face? Yes ___ No ___.

Are you doing what He has asked of you? Yes ___ No ___.

Are you in conflict about what He has asked of you? Yes ___ No ___.

Are you hearing from the Lord Yes ___ No ___.

Write out your concerns that you have and take them to God in prayer.

_____

_____

_____

_____

_____

_____

_____

_____

_____

_____

_____

_____

_____

_____

_____

_____

_____

_____

_____

_____

_____

_____

_____

_____

If most of your answers are yes, then continue to work on your goals and do not hesitate to allow the Lord to tweak your goals. If most answers are no, ask the Lord to show you yourself and what's keeping you from hearing from Him. Then strengthen yourself in His Word.

Write out your thoughts

_____

_____

_____

_____

_____

_____

_____

_____

_____

_____

_____

_____

_____

_____

_____

_____

_____

_____

_____

_____

_____

_____

_____

_____

_____

_____

_____

If you do not know Jesus as your Lord and Savior you can this very moment, *"That if thou shalt confess with thy mouth the Lord Jesus, and shalt believe in thine heart that God hath raised him from the dead, thou shalt be saved. For with the heart man believeth unto righteousness; and with the mouth confession is made unto salvation."* Romans 10:9-10.

Ask the Lord Jesus to come into your heart. Believe that He has, then go and tell somebody. And may the Lord God bless you in all your endeavors.

References

American Heritage Dictionary. (1983). Boston, MA: Houghton Mifflin Company.

Amplified Bible Expanded Edition, (1987), Grand Rapids, MI: Zondervan Publishing House.

Domestic Violence Duluth Model: Online URL www.theduluthmodel.org/wheelgallery.php

Evans, A.T. (2009). Tony Evans Book of Illustrations. Chicago, Il: Moody Publishers.

Feder, L. (1999). Women and Domestic Violence: An Interdisciplinary Approach. New York: Haworth Press.

Gordon, L. (2002). Heroes of their Own Lives. Urbana IL: University Press., p. 253.

Green, N. (1989). Criminals Law Reports: Being reports of cases Determined in the Federal and state courts of the United States.

Greif, G., & Ephross, P. H. (1997). Group Work With Populations At Risk. New York, Oxford: Oxford University Press.

Gruen, A. (1995). Building Self-Esteem. New York: Crossroad Publishing

Gruen, A. (2000). Building Self-Esteem The Christian Dimension. New York: Crossroad Publishing Co.

House of Common Sitting. (1973). Battered Women. Hansard. millbanksystem.com

Kleinberg, S.J. (1999). <u>Women in the United States</u>, 1830-1945. Rutgers University Press., p. 143.

McAuliffee & McAuliffee. (1975). <u>The Essentials of Chemical Dependency</u>.

Minneapolis, Minn: American Chemical Dependency Society.

Nee, W. (1968). <u>The Spiritual Man</u>. New York: Christian Fellowship Publishers, Inc.

New Living Translation Bible. (1997). Wheaton, IL.: Tyndale House Publishers, Inc.

<u>New International Version Study Bible</u> (1995), Grand Rapids, MI: Zondervan Publishing House.

Shipman. (2004). Domestic Violence is known as . . . Wikipedia free encyclopedia. En.wikipedia.org

Swindoll, C. (2010). <u>Because of You</u>: <u>Celebrating The Difference You Make</u>, Compendium Incorporated. Complied by Zadra, and Lambert.

Torrey, R. A. (1971). <u>The Power of Prayer</u>. Grand Rapids, MI: Zondervan Publishing House.

Werner, H. D. (1982). <u>Cognitive Therapy: A Humanistic Approach</u>. New York: Free Press.

Zodhiates, S. Th.D. (1984). <u>The Hebrew-Greek Study Bible with Lexical Aids</u>. Chattanooga, TN: AMG Publishers

About the Author

Brenda Leffall McGibboney is a widow, a mother and grandmother of two adult children, and two grandchildren. Brenda is from the great state of Texas, Dallas is her hometown. She has lived in various parts of the United States, but now makes Greensboro, North Carolina her home. Brenda has earned a bachelor of Social Work (BSW), from North Carolina Agricultural and Technical State University, in Greensboro, North Carolina, and a Master of Social Work (MSW), from University of South Carolina, in Columbia South Carolina. Brenda has many life experiences which she use to help advocate for those who are hurting and abused in life. She has worked in shelters with families of domestic violence, worked in mental health facilities, and extensive work with families in crises. She recently retired as a social worker working with families in Child Protective Services. Brenda published her first book last year, titled Come and Dine with Me, which is listed with Amazon. com, Barnes and Noble and other book distributors. Brenda is a licensed Evangelist/Missionary working with outreach ministries in her local church and a Sunday School teacher.

Brenda is the Founder/President of Renewal Center for Battered Women Ministries, Inc. This ministry was Holy Spirit inspired. The Lord Jesus Christ who wants His people to know that they have the cure to stop domestic violence in their lives. There is hope, and that hope is in Christ Jesus.